chosen
by God

chosen
a brother's journey by God

Joshua Hammer

NEW YORK

Designed by Ruth Lee

Library of Congress Cataloging-in-Publication Data

Hammer, Joshua.
    Chosen by God : a brother's journey / Joshua Hammer.
        p. cm.
    ISBN 0-7868-6428-1
    1. Hammer, Joshua.—Family. 2. Jews—New York (State)—
Family relationships. 3. Hammer, Tuvia. 4. Hasidim—New York
(State)—Monsey—Biography. 5. Brothers—New York (State)—
Biography. 6. Hammer family. 7. Jews—Return to Orthodox Judaism.
8. New York (State)—Biography.   I. Title.
F130.J5H36   1999
974.7'004924'0092—dc21   99-15570
                                CIP

Paperback ISBN 0-7868-8601-3

FIRST PAPERBACK EDITION

10 9 8 7 6 5 4 3 2 1

acknowledgments

WRITING THIS BOOK WOULD not have been possible without the help and encouragement of many people. Michael Maren and Dani Shapiro first planted the idea in my head on a summer night in 1997 and remained strongly supportive throughout the two years it took to bring it to fruition. Hershey Felder, a former yeshiva *bucher* himself, provided guidance and invaluable editorial suggestions at many stops along the way. Thanks also to John Taylor, Andrew Purvis, Gretchen Lang, Donatella Lorch, John Balzar, Vivienne Walt, Jeff Schaeffer, Philip Gourevitch, David Van Biema, Bill Stadiem, Kathleen Hughes, Andrew Murr, John McAlevey, Shem Bitterman, Ted Blumberg, Elizabeth Greenberg, Patti Hammer, Jim and Lois Ullman, Joe and Barbara Ruskin, and the *Newsweek* library research staff. I also want to thank my editors at *Newsweek*, including Ann McDaniel, Michael Glennon, Michael Elliott, Jon Meacham, Mark Whitaker, and the late, much-missed Maynard Parker, for the terrific opportunities they've given me all over the world during the last decade, and for granting me the time to complete this project. My agent Flip Brophy at Sterling Lord Literistic, and my editor Leigh Haber at Hyperion were always available to listen to my anxious ramblings and to offer their reassurance and cogent advice. My father, mother, and step-mother, Arlene, despite some initial—and understandable—hesitation, came on board early on and became allies, joggers of my memory, and invaluable sources of historical information.

My brother Tuvia, sister-in-law Ahuva, and their family opened up their lives and their home to me, listened to my endless questions, fed me wonderfully, and asked for nothing in return. I am eternally grateful to them. *L'chaim.*

Finally, and most of all, I want to thank Helen Palmer for her love and support. Without her inexhaustible patience, literary gifts, generosity of spirit, and strength of character, I would still be huddled over my laptop computer, struggling to find the way through the labyrinth.

M Y BROTHER STANDS BESIDE ME IN THE BASE-ment synagogue, his bearded face glistening beneath harsh fluorescent lighting. Silently he cloaks himself in a silver-brocaded shawl and thumbs through a tattered prayer book to the evening service. Murmurs from the other shrouded worshipers percolate around him, little geysers of sound that seem to spin off in a dozen directions. As the rabbi rises to face the Ark of the Torah, the men stand and blend their voices together as one rushing stream of prayer.

My brother's eyes are tightly shut now. He tilts his head slightly forward, then back, the soft Hebrew syllables tumbling easily from his lips. It's not a strong voice, rather thin and reedy, with a tendency to break at the higher notes, yet it resonates with such soulfulness that it isn't unpleasant to hear. As he prays, he begins to bend at the waist with robotic movements, jerky flexes that seem to bring him close to a state of rapture. Then, all at once, he punctuates his wail with a half dozen sharp blows against the right side of his chest. The harsh thumping against his heart makes me wince.

I watch my brother, transfixed, repelled by his act of self-surrender, and amazed at the depth of his emotion. His fervor seems to reach back across oceans and generations, linking my brother with our ancestors in the shtetls of the Ukraine, with the nomads of the Sinai desert. Eyelids pressed together, lips pulled back, straining to concentrate every part of his being on the Creator, the little brother I grew up with has been transported to a distant place, and I realize I will never get him back.

chosen
by God

FOR THE BETTER PART OF TWO DECADES, I almost never saw nor spoke to my younger brother. Although we had grown up together, played together on the streets of New York City, and suffered through the trauma of our parents' painful divorce, the rift between us had grown so wide by early adulthood that most people who knew me figured that I was an only child.

The break had come shortly after Tony turned twenty-one, when my brother seemed to shed his personality like an old skin. It was at that time that he decided to devote his life to God. He proclaimed himself to be a "Torah Jew"—identifying himself with the ultra-Orthodox fringe of Judaism, whose adherents maintain that every word of the Old Testament is the literal truth and isolate themselves as much as possible from the secular world. He professed the beliefs that God created heaven and earth 5,750 years ago, parted the Red Sea, and revealed the Torah to the Israelites on top of Mount Sinai. He avowed that the Jews are God's chosen people, and that their principal obligation in this world is to bring themselves closer to the Almighty and proclaim His glory. His life was governed by the 613 *mitzvahs*, or divine commandments enumerated in the Torah, which regulate all facets of one's existence—from eating to bathing to sexual relations. Unlike modern Orthodox Jews—whose acceptance of the Torah as the word of God goes together with a firm embrace of the temporal world—my brother regarded secularism as philosophically incompatible with his religious values, and he set out to build a life apart.

For years my brother's religious transformation filled me with a rage and embarrassment so profound that even today I struggle to understand it. I had always hoped that Tony would find a focus—he had always seemed dissatisfied, searching—but ultra-Orthodox Judaism was never what I had in mind. His embrace of fundamentalism marked a total rejection of who our family was—secular, liberal agnostics. I regarded his metamorphosis as a sign of psychological weakness, and even felt disgusted by his surrender to what I viewed as blind faith. Most repugnant, I felt, was the exclusionary nature of that faith—an oft-expressed disdain for homosexuals, African Americans, Reform Jews, and gentiles that found its justification, according to my brother, in the words of the Torah.

As we grew older, my brother and I drifted further and further apart. By the time I reached my late thirties, we had become something like mirror opposites: I was an unmarried foreign correspondent. My brother worked in various part-time jobs and had six children—three boys and three girls—ranging between twelve and two years old. I had lived on four continents in four years and in many ways thrived on the fact that I had no idea where I'd be two years hence. My brother had rarely strayed from his community, and his future seemed etched in stone. As I reported on bodies piled high in Rwandan churches, child killers in Liberia, paramilitary death squads in Colombia, the very idea of God seemed like an indulgence. To my brother, worshiping God was the very point of human existence. Contemplating his life was like staring into a fun house mirror and seeing oneself reflected back in a reversed, wildly distorted image. The more I thought about him, the more intrigued I found myself becoming by the common psychological denominators that seemed to underpin our divergent lives. My shame about my brother was beginning to go hand in hand with a nagging curiosity.

The years passed, and my anger abated, slowly. Separated from him by many thousands of miles, I contemplated reestablishing contact with him. My motives were located at the nexus where blood, emotion, curiosity, ambition, and self-interest collide. I had spent years covering alien societies in Africa, poking into unfamiliar rituals and customs. In a similar way, I had begun to regard my brother and his community with a kind of journalistic detachment, rather than with full-blooded visceral aversion. Eventually, I even considered writing—a magazine article, a book—about his transformation. The project did not appeal to me merely because it was a potentially gripping story. It was only by approaching him through the cold eyes of a journalist, I felt, that I could find a way to repair a rift and restore a semblance of completeness to my family.

In the fall of 1997, I decided to move back to America after five years overseas. It seemed like an appropriate time to break the silence. One rainy afternoon, from my office in downtown Buenos Aires, I called my brother's house in the suburban village of Monsey, New York, and spoke to his wife, Ahuva— whom he had married fourteen years earlier, following a *shidduch*, or match, set up by members of his community. At first startled by my phone call, she quickly warmed up to me and invited me to visit the family on my next trip to New York. In my mind, it would be an exploratory journey—to see how my brother had changed, to make an overture, to discover if his world and our relationship were worth probing in depth. Then, on the Sunday of Thanksgiving weekend, after turkey sandwiches and NFL football at my father's Manhattan apartment, I telephoned my brother and heard his voice for the first time in five years. We exchanged pleasantries, and I scribbled down the directions to his house.

"I'll see you around three o'clock?"

"Three o'clock," he replied.

My father regarded me fixedly as I hung up the phone. "You're really going through with this?" he asked. One bond we had always shared was a sense of embarrassment and regret about my brother's life. My father scornfully called him "the Rabbi," and, like me, had shunned him over the years. He didn't think my writing about Tony and our family was a good idea. He didn't want the past dredged up. I sensed that he regarded my overtures to Tony as a kind of betrayal.

It was a chilly, windy afternoon. I picked up my rental car on East Ninety-second Street, and headed north along the FDR Drive toward the George Washington Bridge. I was nervous, wondering how Tony's life might have changed over the last half decade, wondering if he bore me any ill will for the long silence between us. Under a slate gray sky, the Hudson River was a slow-flowing torrent that meandered past the towering New Jersey cliffs, a scene of pastoral tranquility on Manhattan's edge that was momentarily soothing.

Crossing the bridge, I turned north toward Rockland County, the hotbed of New York's ultra-Orthodox population, where a hundred thousand or so observant Jews dwell in a cluster of suburban villages thirty miles north of New York City. Baseball diamonds and ranch houses peeked through thick stands of oak and maple trees along the highway. Forty minutes after leaving Manhattan, I turned off the Palisades Parkway at Spring Valley, a down-at-the-heels suburb of scruffy Victorian houses and strip malls. My heart beat a little quicker at the imminent prospect of seeing Tony. Remembering the sadness and anger I had felt during the last trip to Monsey five years earlier, I fought off another impulse to make a U-turn, out of my brother's life forever.

Monsey announced itself with a flash of black: a Hasidic yeshiva boy raced across the street, *peyyes* flapping. Signs in both Hebrew and English adorned the facades of tidy shops on Main Street: Krausz Hatter, Monsey Glatt Kosher Wok, Kosher Komputer, "for all your Judaical software needs." Following the directions I had scribbled on a yellow Post-it note, I drove down a leafy street lined with ramshackle wood-shingle and brick bungalows, and stopped before the third house from the end.

My first reaction to the scene was a mixture of shock and dismay. I remembered that my brother lived in humble circumstances, but the little red brick house, set against the relative tidiness of the other homes on the block, seemed almost a caricature of neglect. My eyes were assaulted from a dozen different directions. Chest-high piles of damp cardboard boxes filled with rotting leaves teetered at the curbside. I glanced past the boxes, over the small bare brown lawn to the brick house itself. The wooden porch seemed lopsided. Torn window screens had been patched over with duct tape, and the number 62 dangled in broken fragments from the lintel. Square pots filled with bedraggled petunias hung from hooks beside the front door.

I slammed the car door shut, pushed open a gate in a rickety wire fence, and descended three stone steps to the lawn. I was overwhelmed with a sense of disorder. Dozens of broken toys littered the yard, like colorful debris washed up by the tide. I walked past a half-deflated toddler's pool filled with orange water and dead leaves, and nearly tripped over a red plastic fire engine missing its front wheels.

Hoping that I had come to the wrong house, I walked hesitantly up the wooden steps leading to the porch. At that moment a figure dressed in black stepped through the front door. I froze, studying the vision in front of me. A shapeless black coat draped his body to his ankles. A wide-brimmed black hat covered his head, and his features were almost completely concealed behind a wild bird's nest of a beard that dangled in uncombed strands nearly a foot below his chin, like a biblical prophet's. In his arms he held his daughter—one of two children born since the last time I'd seen him—a blond-haired two-year-old who regarded me wide-eyed. I stared in astonishment at the eighteenth-century apparition before me. The last time I had seen him, in the winter of 1993, he had been neatly attired in a black fedora and dark business suit, the standard uniform of the Americanized ultra-Orthodox Jews. But he had cast off that look for this more extreme incarnation, and I was not sure what to make of it.

"*Shalom aleichem,*" my brother said.

WHENEVER PEOPLE ASK ME ABOUT MY BROTH-er's transformation, I always start the story in the same place: Israel. In the fall of 1980, as my brother planned the journey that would change his life forever, he was a nineteen-year-old college junior seized, like so many people his age, by an insatiable wanderlust and a desire to change the world. In many ways my brother was an impressive young man: an accomplished undergraduate actor and an aspiring political activist, torn between dreams of a career on Broadway or the Beltway. Yet as he stood on the cusp of adulthood, in truth my brother was also probably something of a misfit. He could appear painfully nervous and insecure. He was eager to be taken seriously, but some of his friends called him "goofy" and "clownish." He seemed desperate to be loved, but couldn't get a date. He was always searching for gurus, and though he was intellectually curious, he could never seem to focus on anything for long. One thing was certain: religion held no interest for him. Like me, Tony had been raised with some awareness of his Jewish roots, but hadn't set foot inside a synagogue since his bar mitzvah.

That fall, in a political philosophy course at Hobart College in upstate New York, Tony seized upon a new intellectual hero: Karl Marx. In December he persuaded the financial aid department at Hobart to lend him $1,000 and a round-trip plane ticket to Tel Aviv for a program of "independent study" that he had conjured up himself. In Israel, he told our father, he would live the socialist ideal on a kibbutz and study German so he could read *Das Kapital* in the original.

"Of all the places to learn German, why go to Israel?" our father demanded.

"A lot of Israelis speak German," Tony retorted.

"They're concentration camp survivors. You think they're going to teach you German?"

"Then I'll teach myself."

A former *New York Times* reporter and award-winning author, our father was a tough and demanding man, with expectations that his sons would follow steady courses toward successful careers. He seemed to trust me implicitly—I had graduated from Princeton with honors, and was fairly clear about my writing ambitions—but he had little patience for Tony's capricious nature, his disorganization, his enthusiasms that petered out as quickly as they took hold. Although he seemed to admire Tony's intellectual energy and acting talent, he viewed my brother as an easily intoxicated, easily distracted child who needed a firm guiding hand. His criticism tended to make my brother even more defiant.

Tony landed at Ben-Gurion Airport on a freezing morning just after New Year's Day in 1981. He was euphoric, judging from the tone of his letters to me and our parents, full of a young man's wonder at seeing the wider world for the first time. But after one night in a Tel Aviv youth hostel, Tony abruptly abandoned his plans to live on a kibbutz. He signed up instead as a volunteer on a private farm, or *moshav*, on the West Bank. Unlike a kibbutz, he explained, the moshav permitted one to live in close contact with an Israeli family—in this case, a couple in their thirties, both veterans of the 1967 War. He moved into a spartan dormitory with young adventurers from Europe and went to work, driving a tractor and picking grapes, strawberries, and corn from dawn to dusk along the irrigated banks of the Jordan River.

It all sounded pretty good. He was teaching himself Hebrew at night, picking up Arabic from a Palestinian co-worker. While reading Leon Uris's *Exodus,* he said, he had begun to identify with the Jewish settlers who had carved the state of Israel out of the semi-desert two generations earlier. Still, he remained resolute in his skepticism about religion. "The Promised Land was delivered not by some greater Being, but through the sweat and blood of the Jews," he declared. "I am now infected with an insatiable desire to see the rest of Israel."

After two weeks, however, Tony changed course once again. He wrote to our father to say he had rented an apartment in Jerusalem with a seventeen-year-old Israeli named Ronnie, whom he had met on the farm. There had been too little privacy to study Marx and write poetry in the dorm, he explained. He had found a job washing dishes at night and was spending his days reading, writing, and exploring the city. "All I can say now is that Israel is remarkable. Israel is a brother, a father, a mother, and a home for me."

Fragments of Tony's adventure would make their way to me at various post offices in Asia—Bangkok, Jakarta, Katmandu, Karachi. I had finished a year-long teaching fellowship in Tokyo and was backpacking across the continent, enjoying a last taste of freedom before returning to America. Both Tony and I were wanderers that year. But in contrast to his criticism of my brother's trip to Israel, our father was ecstatic about my overseas adventure. In our father's eyes I had a clear goal: gathering exotic experiences that would serve me well in my future writing career. I would be home soon. Tony was anointed "the loser," adrift, lacking direction. Who knew when—or if—he planned to come back to America?

Tony's love affair with Israel had all happened too fast, our father wrote. "Tony has that penchant for leaping into something new with both feet and total commitment at the beginning and then, too soon, turning aside and finding something new to captivate him. We can only hope that he begins to find some direction in his life," he wrote. He asked me to try to visit Tony on my way back to the United States and determine his state of mind. I had already been considering reconnecting with my brother in Israel. Cast in the role of our father's emissary, I felt seized by an additional sense of mission.

On a warm spring afternoon in 1981, after a week of hitchhiking through Greece, I flew from Athens to Tel Aviv, landing at Ben-Gurion Airport in the early evening darkness. I was thrilled by the sight of soldiers everywhere—swarthy young men wearing little knit yarmulkes and carrying Galil rifles slung over their shoulders. The Camp David peace accords had recently been signed, but Israel was still surrounded by enemies. I felt an unexpected surge of Jewish identity when confronted with these fellow Jews under siege.

A pedestrian guided me down a flight of stone steps and into the unlit streets of the old Nachla'ot neighborhood. I found my way to a two-story apartment block at the bottom of a steep alley. A label with the name *T. Hammer* was stuck on the door of a ground-floor apartment. I knocked. I heard the strumming of a guitar, and then stared into the face of a young, bearded stranger.

"*Ken?*" he asked, in Hebrew.

"I'm looking for Tony Hammer."

He looked me up and down, and asked: "Are you Josh?"

"That's right."

He smiled. "I'm Ronnie. I'm his roommate."

"Ronnie," I said, shaking his hand, starting to feel at home. "My brother mentioned you in his letters. Is he around?"

"He works at night. I'll take you there."

We strolled together down Jaffa Road, Jerusalem's main shopping street, through lively crowds to Fefferberg's, a kosher delicatessen humming with energetic conversation; white-jacketed waiters bustled to and fro, balancing trays laden with towering pastrami and corned beef sandwiches. My brother was standing at the busboy station just past the entrance, wearing a stained white smock, carrying a tub of dirty dishes. We spotted each other simultaneously.

"Oh, my God," he said, sinking theatrically to the floor. "I'm in total shock."

His friends were right, I thought. He was goofy. And skinny, I noticed, with an unhealthy pallor. He had a bad cough, and his face was blotched with acne. We hadn't seen each other and had hardly spoken in eighteen months. After my often lonely odyssey through Asia, I was elated to set eyes on him.

"My God," my brother said. "You almost gave me a heart attack. How come you didn't give me any warning?"

"You don't have a telephone."

"That's true. Are you planning to stay for a while?"

"A couple of weeks. Dad asked me to check up on you."

My brother laughed. "He's worried about me, huh?"

My brother and Ronnie shared a railroad-style flat on the ground floor of a two-story building in a working-class neighborhood a few blocks west of the Old City. I was immediately struck by the place's squalor. It was no typical undergraduate's crash pad: a mountain of filthy dishes filled the kitchen sink, spilling over onto counters, piling up on the chipped linoleum floor. Layers of congealed tomato sauce and other food particles covered the gas stove. The sink was overflowing with a black ooze, on which floated a flotsam of foodstuffs, soggy paper, fruit rinds, and fruit pits. There was a strong, sweet smell of decay.

Ronnie slept in the living room. Tony's room was at the back of the apartment. It stank of dirty clothing. On a mattress in the corner of the small space lay a crumpled sleeping bag. A stack of cardboard boxes, appropriated from a liquor store, served as a dresser. The scuffed white walls were bare. A broken door, laid on its side and balanced on piles of cement blocks, functioned as a desk. Sheets of notebook paper, underwear, Halvah wrappers, and dirty plates lay strewn around the room. "I've been pretty busy," he said, kicking a four-foot-high pile of laundry aside and laying down a spare mattress on the floor. "I should probably do a wash."

My brother's squalid living conditions quickly confirmed the worst to me: he was lost. Certainly I was inclined to view my brother in the most negative light—to confirm my own superiority in our father's eyes, and place myself in the role of sibling rescuer. In retrospect, perhaps his life had not derailed as completely as it then seemed. Still, there were objective signs of extreme disorder. He and Ronnie, who earned a few shekels a day playing guitar in the Armenian quarter of the Old City, lived like scavengers. Half their time seemed to be spent foraging for food. At times they were reduced to searching the city's open-air markets for discarded fruits and vegetables, jostling with old ladies for the rotting, crushed tomatoes and strawberries that lay on the ground at closing time. They tore up free tourist maps of

Jerusalem to use as toilet paper. Their neighbors wanted them evicted. They would constantly borrow things—a corkscrew, a plunger—and forget to return them or misplace them for weeks. Ronnie's girlfriend and a dozen other teenage friends would drop by, smoke marijuana or hashish, eat rice and beans from communal pots, and blast music at full volume till the early hours of the morning.

At the beginning, at least, we got along fine. In the early mornings we wandered through the buzzing Damascus Gate into the Arab Quarter of the Old City, a ten-minute walk from Hammadregot Street, passing grizzled men in *kefiyehs* and Arab boys herding heavily laden mules. We lost ourselves in shadowy alleyways where tinny Middle Eastern music wafted from shortwave radios, and rummaged through spice and curio shops. At an outdoor Arab café a stone's throw from the Dome of the Rock, we spent hours talking over cheap plates of hummus and olives, cups of sweetened cardamom tea, and a hookah filled with Turkish tobacco. We explored the dank Catacombs beneath the Western Wall, climbed the Mount of Olives to sit in the Jewish cemetery and view the arid hills and ancient dun-colored ramparts glowing in the late afternoon sunlight. On crisp spring mornings in the Old City, as we passed the water pipe back and forth, listening to the coffee-colored water bubbling as we breathed in the pungent smoke, I felt as close to him as I had in my life. I had never been entirely comfortable around my brother; I felt threatened by his intellectual energy, yet at the same time shrank from what I regarded as his sometimes naked insecurity. But during those idylls in the Arab Quarter, the dark subtext of our relationship seemed to fade away. We were siblings, reunited in an exotic place, far from our parents, joined together by our sense of freedom and our youth.

I told him about my year as an English teacher and film critic for an English language newspaper in Tokyo, and my subsequent nine months of travel through Southeast Asia, India, and the Himalayas. I described the joys of trekking for seven weeks through the most spectacular landscape on the planet, and the terrors of being attacked by a drunken, paint-throwing mob of celebrants in the alleys of Varanasi, India's holiest city, built along the Ganges River. I talked about riding a bus through the Khyber Pass to the Afghan frontier, and listening to the thuds of artillery fire at night as I lay in a hammock on a rooftop in the border town of Torkham. At twenty-three, I no longer had ambitions of becoming a playwright, as I'd contemplated at Princeton. I wanted to be a journalist, like our father, to travel and have adventures and write about them.

My brother seemed to have a different ambition each day. He dreamed of being a poet. He talked of setting up an experimental theater company in Jerusalem. One day he couldn't wait to return to study at Hobart College. The next he wanted to renounce his American citizenship and settle permanently in Israel.

The closeness between us didn't last. In retrospect, I see that I had come to Israel predisposed to find fault with my brother's life. Instead of giving him any credit for undertaking an adventure in a foreign place, I began to rub his nose in his "shortcomings" with a certain grim relish; I wrote several detailed aerogrammes to my father describing Tony's hacking cough, filthy kitchen, and regular intake of marijuana. The letters drew my father and me closer into a conspiratorial bond against Tony: "Please don't let him know that I'm passing on this information to you," I pleaded. I clashed frequently with my brother's lackadaisical roommate, whom Tony insisted was a genius, a Left Bank–style artiste, "the most intellectual human being I've ever known."

Then there was "Jack," a homeless woman who would drift through the apartment periodically, two young daughters in tow.

Jack was a chain-smoking Englishwoman whose life was contained in a cluster of plastic shopping bags. We never got along. I came to regard Jack as one more element of confusion in Tony's life. I began to relish a confrontation with her: it was, I can see in retrospect, partly out of a genuine concern for my brother's welfare, partly out of a desire to assert myself as my brother's keeper, a paragon of responsibility and maturity. One night two weeks into my stay, I decided she had to go.

"I think you should leave," I said as we all sat together, sharing a pot of spaghetti.

"I don't think that's your decision," said Ronnie sharply.

I ignored him. "You can stay the night, but that's it."

Jack stared at me. "What gives you the right—"

"What gives you the right to treat your kids this way?"

"Who are you?" she said.

"Who am I? Who are *you?*"

Ronnie attempted to intervene, told her that she was still welcome here, and told me I was out of line. But it didn't matter. By dawn the next morning Jack and her children were gone. Ronnie and I rarely exchanged another word. My brother was furious at my interference.

"I'm just trying to get you on the right track," I said.

"Try to go five minutes," he told me, "without telling us how to live."

NEARLY EVERY MORNING WHILE I WAS IN JErusalem, I would stroll through the bustling Jaffa Gate of the Old City and plunge into the Arab *shook*, where old men in kefiyehs smoked hookahs on the stoops of carved wooden doorways, and one-eyed and limbless beggars gazed at me with plaintive stares and outstretched palms. Wandering through stone-walled alleys cast in perpetual shadow, I would hurry past the butcher stalls, where the bloody hinds of cows and sheep and camel's heads hung from rusting hooks, and inhale with pleasure the sweet aromas wafting from bins of coffee, cardomom, cumin, turmeric, and thyme. I would pass through a crumbling stone archway built during the time of Jesus Christ, descend a steep staircase and emerge into the sweeping plaza before the holiest shrine in all of Judaism: the Western Wall, the sole remnant of the First and Second Temples of the Israelites.

The first time I saw the Wall, the experience was even more powerful than I had anticipated. The ruin was only five stories tall—yet it seemed to possess a concentrated grandeur, a sanctity and historical resonance compressed into a surprisingly small space. The huge tan blocks of Herodian stone were set against a liquid blue sky. Dozens of black-clad men bowed reverently before the structure, each worshiper engaged in his own private dialogue with God. I picked up a paper yarmulke from a custodian standing near the Wall and approached, listening to the murmurs of the ultra-Orthodox Jews surrounding me and studying the intricate patterns, ridges and indentations in the stone. Then I stepped back, taking in the plaza, the monumental slabs and, looming majestically behind the Wall, the seventh-century Dome of the Rock atop the Temple Mount—its gilded dome floating on an octagonal base of peacock blue mosaic. I tried to imagine the Second Temple as it had stood two thousand years ago, a vast, teeming complex completely devoted to the worship of God. I imagined the historical actors that had swept across this spot: Babylonian and Roman conquerors, the Crusaders, the Turkish warlord Saladin, the Zionists and their Arab enemies.

Built by King Solomon, the Bais HaMikdash had been a miniature Garden of Eden, a place of absolute spiritual purity. The *shechinah*, God's presence on earth, was said to dwell within its walls. Here generations of Jewish priests, known as *kohenim*, descended from Moses' brother Aharon, burned sacred oil, and carried out gory animal sacrifices in veneration of the Almighty. The First Temple was destroyed by the Babylonians in 586 B.C., and the Jews marched into exile. Sixty-six years later, the Persians conquered Babylon and permitted the Jews to return home and rebuild their holy sanctuary. It stood, unthreatened, for another half millennium. Then, after a three-year siege of Jerusalem, the Roman emperor Titus destroyed the Second Temple in A.D. 70, leaving a single wall standing as a testament to his power. The conquerors marched the Jews into captivity in Rome, starting the *galus*, the current exile, the Jewish people's aliena-tion from their God.

The galus was the central theme of Judaism, I knew: the endless cycle of exile and return, rejection and acceptance by a loving but strict and sometimes cruel God. He was a God who conferred astonishing blessings on the Jews, but who doled out fearsome punishment, lasting for generations, when he sensed that his chosen people had strayed from their obligations. I didn't consider myself a believer—had not been inside a synagogue in the decade since my bar mitzvah—but there was something in-arguably powerful and moving about this. The Wall stood for unshakable faith and thousands of years of tradition, the inex-tinguishability and ultimate ascendance of Judaism after three millennia of persecution and decimation. The sight of the *kosel* Ma'arivi and the ultra-Orthodox Jews kissing the huge blocks and *davening* before it filled me with a sense of awe. Having grown up without religion, I responded to these fervent worshipers with an empathy that took me by surprise. Their lives seemed marked by completeness and certainty, in stark contrast to my own ingrained skepticism. Watching the scene filled me with a longing for harmony, and somehow stirred unwelcome thoughts of the shattering of my family a decade earlier. On my second visit, I turned away from the scene overwhelmed, near tears.

The slim, trimly bearded man with the wire-rim glasses and the black fedora must have seen my eyes glistening. *Tsitsis*, seven knotted strings symbolizing man's commitment to keeping the mitzvahs, dangled from his navy blue suit. He carried a dark leather-bound prayer book as he approached me on the plaza, the heels of his black shoes clicking on the tan cobblestones.

"Excuse me," he said in a strong New York accent. "Do you have the time?"

"Sure," I said. "It's ten o'clock."

He continued to stand there. "Have you got somewhere to go for *Shabbos* this week?"

I shook my head and kept walking. The emotion of a few minutes earlier had dissipated. I was anxious to get away from this Orthodox Jewish proselytizer who had interrupted my reverie.

The following day I saw the man again at the Wailing Wall. I tried to avoid him, but he caught sight of me and hurried after me across the plaza.

"You're Jewish, right? Can I interest you in joining some people for a Shabbos dinner this Friday night?"

"I don't think so," I muttered.

"Some other time?"

I grunted noncommittally. It was one thing to admire Jewish rituals from a safe distance, quite another to be put on the spot like this. Later that evening, back at the apartment on Hammadregot Street, I asked my brother about the man who had accosted me.

"That's Baruch Levine," he told me, with a snicker, as we stood in his grubby kitchen, stirring rice and kidney beans in an enormous black kettle on his sauce-encrusted gas burner. "Watch out for him. First he lures you to a Shabbos dinner, then maybe a visit to the yeshiva; the next thing you know you're wearing a *kipa* and lighting candles. He's come after every American kid who's ever visited the Wall."

Two months earlier, in February, Tony said, setting our unadorned supper down on a low wooden table beside the living room sofa, he had been reading an essay by Marx on some stone steps inside the Old City when Levine had approached him. Levine asked if he would put on *t'fillin*, miniature pieces of the Torah encased in leather boxes and strapped around the forehead and the right arm during prayers. Tony agreed to do it—for reasons he could never explain—and after that Levine rarely left him alone. Under duress Tony agreed to visit a yeshiva. There, he told me, he spent an hour listening to young American students arguing that evolution was a myth, then left in disgust.

"These guys acted as if Darwin had never existed," Tony told me incredulously, spooning out the last globs of food into his plate. I shared his skepticism wholeheartedly. Marx was certainly right, he said, when he described religion as an insidious tool of the upper classes bent on keeping the masses at bay. The experience had left him even more convinced that organized religion was "the opiate of the people."

I was wary of Levine, but it also seemed that I couldn't avoid him; every time I visited the Western Wall, I would spot him patrolling the plaza, on the prowl for impressionable young American Jews. Inevitably, he would find his way to me and resume his sales pitch. He had an ingratiating manner that somehow, day by day, wore down my resistance. One sunny weekday afternoon, Levine ambushed me at the foot of the stairs leading to the plaza; I consented to his offer of a tour through the alleys of the Jewish quarter. As we walked through winding pathways, past modern buildings of tawny sandstone reconstructed after the 1948 War of Independence and the Six-Day War, Levine launched into a paean to the victory of Israeli forces in 1967. "The Arabs turned the Wall into a garbage dump," he said. "When the Israeli troops finally captured it on the sixth day, they wept tears of joy."

On a bright Sunday morning, as a light breeze rippled through the silver-brocaded prayer shawls of the daveners at the Wall, he approached me there and led me on a walk through the Hezekiah's Tunnel, a dank three thousand-year-old passageway that once had linked an underground spring to ancient Jerusalem's main reservoir. The air smelled of mildew and dust and donkey droppings, laced with faint traces of arabica. We took off our shoes, rolled up our pants cuffs, and waded through the ancient aqueduct, our voices echoing off the mossy stones.

"Three old men are marching to the gas chamber, and one of them remembers that today is Simchas Torah," Levine said, referring to the fall festival that celebrates the completion of the year-long cycle of Torah reading. "He tells the others, 'We have to celebrate!' His friends look at him as if he's crazy. But as he begins singing and dancing in line, they join him. The Nazi guards stare at them. They're mystifed—scared. How could these people be so joyful on their way to the death chamber? The Nazis shoot them down, one by one. But the Jews keep dancing, defiant in the face of death, until the end." I wasn't sure I believed Levine's story; it seemed too pat to be the truth. But the young proselytizer's enthusiasm was contagious, and his celebration of Judaism, combined with the antiquity of our surroundings, was having an intoxicating effect on me. I felt mildly drugged, almost giddy. My aversion to Judaism was growing weaker with every step I took along the age-old passageways and footpaths of old Jerusalem.

A trip to Yad Vashem, the Holocaust memorial in the modern city, weakened my defenses further. Huge black-and-white photographs of Nazi death camps, the liquidation of the Warsaw ghetto, *einsatzgruppen* machine gunners standing over trenches filled with murdered Jews in the Ukrainian towns where my ancestors had come from: in the setting of Jerusalem, they seemed to take on even greater power. Emerging from the exhibition, I was consumed by grief, remorse—and a sense of identification. I could not escape from a sense of having abandoned my heritage—my birthright. As we sat in a Jaffa Road café eating falafel one afternoon, I told my brother that I was beginning to reconsider my total abandonment of the Jewish faith.

"I have to confront my heritage and make some decisions," I said.

"I knew it," he said. "Levine's starting to get to you."

He was right. "The problem is," I asked him, "can one be 'a Jew' while still retaining serious doubts about God's existence? Does it make any sense to celebrate the holidays if I'm skeptical of the central tenet of Judaism?"

"Maybe you should stop spending so much time at the Wall," he said with a smile. I found my brother's dismissive attitude annoying; I wondered whether deep down, he was as drawn as I was to Judaism, or even more so.

The next Friday evening, I decided to join Levine for a Shabbos dinner with an ultra-Orthodox family. As sirens wailed from nearby synagogues signaling the time had come to light the Sabbath candles, Tony and I made our way to a prearranged rendezvous spot at the Wall. My brother had decided to accompany me, he said, "to keep an eye on you." I was delighted to have him come along, and took his presence there with me as a sign of his interest; a little dose of religion, I thought, might even be good for him. With three other young American Jews, we followed Levine on foot to Me'a Sha'arim, the city's labyrinthine nineteenth-century Hasidic enclave just outside the Old City ramparts.

Our six-man procession filed through Herod's Gate, and we soon found ourselves in a quarter of serpentine alleys, stately old stone mansions, and tucked-away Judaica shops spilling over with Chanukah menorahs, framed photographs of great Hasidic *rebbes*, bamboo spice holders, polished silver *kiddush* cups. Little boys in peyyes and white yarmulkes, their skin pale to the point of translucence, spilled out of a white-brick yeshiva, chattering in Yiddish. White banners hanging from the sides of buildings warned women in Hebrew and English to "dress and behave modestly" within the religious quarter. We walked up a flight of stairs to a tiny second-floor apartment, and were ushered inside by Rabbi Stefansky, our black-bearded Hasidic host. His wife, an ashen-faced woman in a long print dress and matching head scarf, greeted us shyly, then returned to the kitchen to finish preparing the meal with her daughters. Stefansky gave us a tour of the three rooms: six of his children slept in one. The three youngest shared their parents' master bedroom, and another three slept on the foldout couch in the living room. My brother and I exchanged glances.

The meal went on for three hours, first a procession of heavy eastern European foods served by the women of the house, followed by wine, hard liquor, and joyful singing by the men around the dinner table, arms slung round each other's shoulders. My brother and I stumbled back into the dark alleyways of Me'a Sha'arim, woozy from sweet Israeli wine, schnapps, and amaretto. We followed Levine a few blocks through the labyrinthine alleys of the old ghetto to Toldos Aharon, a synagogue belonging to a highly devout Hasidic sect founded in Jerusalem in the 1920s by an eastern European emigré. We arrived at the shul just before the start of the evening prayer, known as *ma'ariv*.

"Everybody stick together," Levine warned.

Tony and I huddled together in the rear of the cavernous synagogue, transfixed as two hundred long-bearded men cloaked in shimmering gold and blue prayer shawls—the traditional garb of Jerusalem's Hasidim—swayed back and forth before the Ark, the lavishly decorated case found inside every synagogue that contains the Torah scrolls used in services.

I had never seen anything like it. As I cowered beside the door, men turned their faces toward heaven and, literally, screamed. The high-decibel shrieks and moans seemed to emanate from the deepest part of their being, as if they had been possessed by *dybbuks*—the demons of Yiddish folklore. Soon, the worshipers began to shake their bodies violently. They flailed their arms and legs and furiously wagged their heads—two hundred men seized simultaneously by a shared epileptic fit. One mashed his forehead against a wooden pillar. Another collapsed in a heap on the floor.

Afterward, as we stepped back onto the silent street, I felt shaken, awed by a level of religious fervor I had never seen before.

Tony shook his head. "These people want to set humanity back three centuries," he said. I was chagrined that the scene had failed to move him. Perhaps his negative attitude toward Judaism would begin to soften, I thought, under my influence.

The next afternoon, as we sat on the manicured grass by the Old City's ramparts, watching tourists file through the Jaffa Gate, I told my brother that I had accepted Baruch Levine's proposal to spend a week studying in a yeshiva. My interest was more intellectual than emotional. If anything, I was seeking confirmation of what I strongly suspected: that the yeshiva life was too rigid and cloistered for me, and more importantly, its fundamentalist faith was incompatible with my own beliefs. But Tony wasn't convinced. We took a long walk up the Mount of Olives and sat on the hill overlooking the Temple Mount and the ancient serrated ramparts of Jerusalem, waving off the entreaties of Arabs offering us rides on their saddled camels. Bathed in a golden light, the city seemed more seductive than ever.

"I don't think you should do this," he said.

"I don't see how you can have the complete experience of Israel without it."

"They'll deprive you of food and lower your resistance until you can't argue with them. I've seen it happen to people. "

Looking back, I can see that Tony's warning was probably more directed at himself than at me. I had little doubt that I'd handle the yeshiva with the same reportorial detachment that I approached almost everything in my life. But my brother had always been different; Tony perhaps sensed that the yeshiva might sweep him off his feet. My brother's caution was, it seems in hindsight, a self-protective reflex.

Tony began to walk down a stone path through olive groves, past twisted, gnarled trees that seemed as old as the hills themselves, and headed back toward the ancient city. "It's your life," he said patronizingly.

The yeshiva van picked me up at eight o'clock in the morning at the top of the stone steps in Nachla'ot. I was the only passenger. Every few minutes the driver spoke to someone in English at the yeshiva via a two-way radio, giving updates on our progress. Two young scholars, or yeshiva *bucharim*, with identical brown beards, black suits, and yarmulkes, were waiting for me at the gated entrance to the yeshiva in a modern quarter of the city. "We've got a full schedule of classes set up," one said in an American accent, handing me a yarmulke.

Ohr Somayach, Hebrew for "the light of happiness," was one of a half dozen centers of Jewish learning in Jerusalem that catered to *baal tshuvas*—returning Jews or, literally, masters of repentance. A tidy campus of sandstone buildings and gardens, the yeshiva had been founded in 1972 by a multimillionaire Canadian construction magnate named Joseph Tanenbaum. Tanenbaum belonged to the Litvisher sect—one of the two dominant movements of ultra-Orthodox Judaism, along with Hasidism.

Hasidism is a mystical, pietistic movement founded in the mid-eighteenth century by a Polish rabbi known as the Baal Shem Tov. Its practitioners infuse their daily lives with emotional adoration of God—singing, dancing, and engaging in the physically exhausting prayer ritual known as davening—and wear the dangling side locks and long black robes of their ancestors. Litvishers, who trace their roots to the yeshivas of eighteenth-century Lithuania, consider themselves the Hasidim's

"Americanized" cousins. They speak English, wear business suits and neat beards, stress the study of Jewish law, and are not wholly adverse to secular influences.

I felt out of place the moment I walked through the gate. Everywhere I looked, *baal tshuvas* were scurrying off to lectures and seminars—a sea of bearded young men who seemed swept up by spiritual intoxication. Many, I discovered, had been drifters and seekers who had ventured to the Himalayas or ashrams in India and eventually made their way to Israel. Nearly all had been accosted by Baruch Levine or one of his cohorts at the Wailing Wall. You could see the struggles going on within them: about half had already adopted the somber black suits and ties and neatly barbed beards of the Litvishers. Others clung to the undergraduate look—college sweatshirts, jeans, backpacks—but had stopped shaving and started wearing yarmulkes and tsitsis, the seven white knotted strings dangling from their undergarment that symbolized their commitment to the 613 mitzvahs, or commandments of God, set out in the Torah.

A professor of philosophy started the morning by expounding upon the "sacred covenant" between God and the Jews. Each word of the Torah, he proclaimed, was a complex code that illuminated an indisputable truth: the Jews were chosen by God to proclaim his Oneness and abide by the moral principles specified in the five books of Moses. Then came an hour-long lesson on the Talmud—the fifteen-hundred-year-old compilation of rabbinical dialogues and parables that forms the basis for all Judaic law. By one o'clock, after four hours of listening to such material, my mind was drifting; although I was trying to engage myself, I was finding these Talmudic debates over the division of property and the construction of fortified walls around a city tedious and irrelevant to my life. This environment, I felt, was far more oppressive than anything I had experienced at my Reform temple in Manhattan, decades earlier. The monastic isolation, the unhealthy appearance of the scholars, the apparent unquestioning acceptance of fundamentalist doctrine, the lack of humor—all confirmed to me that the Torah Jews were little different from a cult. When the lunch break arrived, I hustled across a plaza to the cafeteria. My defenses were now firmly in place. A burly red-bearded scholar sat across from me and said a blessing over his plate of chicken, salad, and challah bread. "I haven't seen you around here before," he said.

"I just started today."

"It's nice to see a new face."

A half dozen students gathered. All looked and sounded exactly alike. Where was I from? What did I think of the classes? Had I moved into the dormitory yet? I was staying at my brother's apartment, I told them.

"You should move into the dormitory," one student said.

"I'm pretty comfortable where I am, thanks."

"Leaving the campus at the end of every day dilutes the experience. You need to take in the whole of yeshiva life." The others murmured their assent. Their earnestness, identical appearance, and insistence that I move into the dormitory put me on edge. I was half-convinced that they planned to lure me into their quarters, deprive me of privacy and sleep, bombard me around the clock with talk of God, and break down my resistance.

"We can do a tour of the dorm right after lunch," the student said.

"I think for now I'll stick with the arrangement I've got."

At that moment I spotted a familiar face in the rear of the dining hall. He was an old acquaintance from Princeton. I had met him at the *Daily Princetonian* during freshman year, six years earlier, but had not seen him since. He was sitting alone, reading Hebrew. He looked shockingly pale and gaunt—a shadow of the ebullient college student I remembered. Anxious to escape my fellow students, I walked across the cafeteria to greet him. Gazing up at me with watery eyes, he suddenly remembered who I was and invited me to join him. He had traveled to Israel after freshman year, he told me, and enrolled at Ohr Somayach in 1976. Five years later, he was still living in the dormitory. He did not know when—if ever—he would leave.

"You're happy here?"

"*Baruch Hashem.*" I had heard the phrase several times at the yeshiva; it was a Hebrew expression that meant "Blessed be God." Hashem meant simply "the name." Observant Jews used it in lieu of other words for God, which were considered too holy to be uttered aloud.

"I remember you trying out for the *Princetonian*," I said.

He seemed to look right through me. "That was a long time ago."

I found the encounter frightening. I had barely known this fellow at Princeton, but I remembered him as a budding journalist, a Frisbee player, a typically ambitious assimilated Jew. Seeing him transformed into a hollow-cheeked ascetic, shut away in this claustrophobic environment for a half decade, suddenly made it clear to me that his religious indoctrination was a form of brainwashing. I realized that I viewed his religious commitment not as a positive characteristic but as sign of weakness, the mark of a person who lacked a strong sense of self. I was glad I'd gotten some exposure to yeshiva life, but I now was more certain than ever that I could not continue down this path—it just wasn't for me. I couldn't make the leap of faith that these scholars had made. I couldn't believe that learning the mitzvahs would grant me eternal bliss at the feet of the Almighty in the world to come.

"Are you sure about this?" asked Rabbi Abramoff, the yeshiva's genial South African administrator, when I told him, the following morning, that I'd be departing that afternoon. I lied. I told him I had a commitment to return to the United States. A newspaper job was waiting for me there, I said, and I would lose it if I didn't move quickly.

"The timing was wrong, then."

"Yes," I said, grateful that the rabbi wasn't pushing me to stay.

He brightened. "You know, we have a branch just north of New York City—in a little town called Monsey."

"I'll have to take some more classes there, then."

As I strolled out the gates of the yeshiva into modern Jerusalem, the vibrancy of the city washed over me—the traffic noise, the animated Hebrew conversations, and the smell of falafel. I felt a sense of liberation. The experiment was over. I walked back to my brother's apartment late that afternoon and found him sitting at his desk, immersed in *Das Kapital*. I told him that I wasn't going back to Ohr Somayach, and he looked pleased.

"Thank God," he said. "I was worried about you."

"I still think you should see what it's like," I told him. My own experience had been mind-numbing, and a little chilling. But I believed that a few days in the yeshiva might discipline Tony, open his mind up to his environment, prod him in a new intellectual direction. It might also wean him from his fixation with Marx, which didn't seem to be doing him much good.

"It's not for me," my brother said. I didn't push him further.

On the last adventure of my two-year odyssey overseas, I embarked on a week-long expedition across Israel—a journey back through the millennia to the distant outposts of the ancient Jews. By now I felt as if the spell had been broken, and my pride in my Jewish identity no longer extended to the urge to practice any of the religious rituals. I rode a bus through the barren wastes of the Negev to the Dead Sea, hiked to the top of the age-old Jewish fortress Masada, and slept on the beach in the Israeli-occupied Sinai and ate melons for breakfast that I purchased from nomadic camel herders on the desert shore. I traveled north to the Sea of Galilee and camped with the son of a famous Hollywood screenwriter I met there. The young man now wore a yarmulke and had adopted a Hebrew name. "America seems hollow and empty after a few months in Israel," he told me.

Perhaps, I thought, but I was planning to return home all the same. After two years abroad, my desire to see the world had been sated temporarily; I was not ready to settle into the life of the permanent expatriate, and felt compelled to establish myself on my home ground. Back in Jerusalem, I bought a cheap ticket to London at a Jaffa Road discount travel agency. From there I would fly home to New York. Tony seemed relieved to see me go. And by that point I was glad to be leaving. My brother had become increasingly uncommunicative, and every day we spent together seemed to exacerbate the strain between us. In recent days he'd phoned in sick twice at Fefferberg's after smoking too much hashish with Ronnie in the late afternoon. He was vague about returning to Hobart College for the fall semester. He hadn't written to our parents in four months.

One day Tony received a letter from our father. The tone was perplexed, wounded:

"I hoped that someone who had taken to spending days and nights closed in a small room with the curtains drawn with incense candles burning creating poetry and prose, might find a moment to scribble a line. We love you, we are concerned about you. It seems you have disappeared into the whirlwind."

"Why does he get on my case?" Tony asked.

I couldn't answer him.

• • •

Our father picked me up at Newark Airport on a spring after-noon. Twenty-one months had passed since I was last in the United States, and I drifted through the international terminal as if in a trance. On the drive into Manhattan, we talked of the insanity plea of Reagan's would-be assassin, John Hinckley, the showdown in Poland between Solidarity and the Communist regime, my father's new book project about a financial conspiracy at the Vatican—and my brother.

"How does he seem?" he asked with a tremor in his voice.

"Not so great," I said bluntly. "He's sick. He's broke. He's a mess."

He sighed. Then, with what sounded like a tone of des-peration, he asked, "Did he say anything at all about coming home?"

"He gave me this letter for you," I said, reaching into my day pack and pulling out a crumpled envelope that bore a single word—DAD—written in my brother's childlike script.

My father tore it open eagerly when we arrived at the apartment. "Dear Dad: first, to explain the total absence of cor-respondence: As I already explained to Josh, I have a difficult time writing to people now for the simple reason that I have nothing at this point, I want to say to anyone. I have been accused of being lost, of having no direction. To that I reply that I am young, and still have time to find the right life."

It wasn't much, but it was something. My father dashed off a letter to Israel the next day. "Dear Tony: Josh delivered your letter. At least it let us know you are still among the living. Have you given any thought to how you will return to the United States in time for school? If you cannot because of your circumstances, we would do what we can to get you back here."

My brother did not write back. Weeks went by without a response. A month passed. Two months, and still no word. The dean at Hobart College phoned: Tony, he said, had not sent in the loan applications required for the winter semester. Friends from high school and college called, wondering whether we had heard from him. Three months gone. Then, one Saturday morning just before Labor Day, our mother telephoned me at my apartment. She sounded alarmed. "I just received a letter from Tony," she told me. "He says he's not coming home for a while."

The correspondence was postmarked Jerusalem and dated the last week of August. "Dear Mom," it began. "It's been a while since our last communication, so you may be surprised to hear my plans have changed. I have given up my apartment, and for the past 2½ months I have been living in a yeshiva in Yerushaliyim. I am learning Torah, Gemorah, philosophy and psalms, and I have to admit this is the most intellectually stimulating experience of my life."

On a wintry Friday afternoon in December, as the pallid sun dipped low over the Hudson River, I stood on the bustling corner of Forty-seventh Street and Fifth Avenue, just east of the Midtown diamond district, waiting for the bus that would take me back to my brother's community. There was no signpost for the Monsey Trails commuter express, but the two dozen black-clad men milling about at curbside offered a fair indication that I had come to the right place. A gray-bearded man waving a tattered piece of paper moved among us. He approached and showed me the document: a twenty-year-old doctor's identification card from the Latvian Soviet Socialist Republic.

"Give a little contribution to the medical society?" he asked. "Ten dollars? Today I had ten people give twenty dollars each. We're raising money for a cancer patient. He's dying of cancer. Won't you give something?"

I handed him a dollar, and he moved on.

A month had passed since my first encounter with my brother in his home after returning from overseas. That brief meeting had raised more questions than it had answered. We had sat in his dark, austere living room for an hour, talking about our family while his baby daughter, Gnendi, played on the rug. My brother had been shockingly vicious—attacking our father for his second marriage to a non-Jew, making hostile comments about Christmas, and referring to Jesus by the disparaging name Yoshka. He had spat in contempt and said that Christ was "*a shaygess* and a *mumzer*," Yiddish for "a bum and a bastard." I had come close to walking out after the first fifteen minutes of conversation, so alarmed was I by his venom. Why was he so angry? I wondered. Where were his wife and children? Why was the house in such terrible shape? I was startled by the ferocity of what appeared to be his deepening religious extremism, by the sense of neglect in the house, and by his all-consuming fundamentalist fire. Yet at the same time, after suppressing my curiosity about him for so long, my journalistic instincts were awakening. I was suddenly intrigued by the arcane rituals of his life, the insular community in which he lived, the complexities of his psychological metamorphosis, and his relationship with a shadowy Hasidic rabbi whom my mother had mentioned to me on her visit to Africa three years earlier. Days after my initial visit, I had called my brother again and proposed that I spend some time in Monsey with him and his family. He was hesitant at first, admitting he was concerned about the impact I might have on his children. But I assured him that I would live by his rules, and he invited me to spend another weekend with his family in Monsey the next time I passed through New York.

The throng surged forward as the three-thirty P.M. bus pulled up to the curb, and the driver—a young Hasid with pencil-thin peyyes—leapt out to hurry passengers aboard and stash their luggage below. I paid my six-dollar fare and settled into a seat at the back. Beating the commuter rush, we sped through the Lincoln Tunnel and north across suburban New

Jersey. The sounds of Yiddish, Argentine Spanish, and English washed over me as I leafed through *The New York Times*. Arriving in Monsey, the bus wound up hills, past new housing developments sprouting from clearings in the woods.

The daylight had started to fade. At each stop groups of passengers clambered into the street, bidding farewell to each other and the driver with a hearty "Good Shabbos." The bus snaked through quiet, maple-lined streets until it reached the corner of Carlton and Blauvelt Roads, and deposited me directly in front of my brother's home.

I was immediately surrounded. Three small boys wheeled around me excitedly as I rolled my suitcase across the street. They were my brother's three sons: Yosef Dov, eleven, Yankel, nine, and Dovid, seven, all wearing identical black-and-white-checked vests and black felt skullcaps. Their hair was closely cropped and curling, feathery strands of blondish hair hung below their ears.

"You didn't bring the dogs?" asked Yosef Dov, peering through broken horn-rimmed glasses held together by masking tape. He seemed eager, awkward. He reminded me a little of myself when I was eleven years old.

"Dogs?"

"*Tateh* says you have big dogs." The word was Yiddish for "dad."

"They don't like flying on airplanes."

"Tateh says that someday we can go on an airplane," he said, leading me by the hand to the living room. In the murky half-light, I could make out a few pieces of old furniture, a glass-doored cabinet containing silver candelabra and fancy china, framed photographs of white-bearded rabbis staring benignly from the walls, and bookshelves filled with Hebrew tomes. From the far corner, a twenty-gallon goldfish tank glowed through the gloom.

My brother walked through the front door moments later, back from a long day studying at the kollel. "Hello, *kinderlach*," he cried. The three boys gathered excitedly around their father, joined by their sister Ruchel, twelve, and Gnendi, three, beaming angelically. Ahuva, my brother's wife, followed them from the kitchen, carrying her wailing baby, Dina Gittel. She wished me a good Shabbos, keeping her distance. I was immediately overwhelmed by an unfamiliar sensation of family closeness. But I was reminded of my status as an observer as I watched my brother and his family set about performing the rituals that would usher in the Sabbath.

At precisely eighteen minutes before sundown, as stipulated by the laws of the Torah, the eight members of his family gathered around a low table beside the window for the lighting ceremony. Silently my brother set down a tarnished brass candleholder containing ten white tapered candles—one for each member of his family, two representing the mitzvahs particular to the Sabbath, refraining from work and consecrating the day with wine. As Ahuva lit the candles with a kitchen match, my brother tilted his head toward the heavens and sang the Sabbath prayer. The dining room was now darkening quickly,and the flickering light of the candles danced across his children's faces. "*Baruch atah adonoi,*" he intoned. My brother elongated each syllable, investing each Hebrew word with quavering intensity, turning what I remembered from childhood as a fifteen-second recitation into a soaring incantation perhaps five times as long. With a final burst of exertion he soared toward the climax. "*She-e-el Sha-a-bbos.*"

The hamlet was now effectively sealed off from the world. No cars moved through its streets. The phones had stopped ringing. The entire community of 30,000 observant Jews— Hasidim and Americanized ultra-Orthodox—Sephardim and Ashkenazim—scattered over several square miles of rolling hills and leafy suburban lanes—had reverted to the pre-industrial age. For the next twenty-four hours, Monsey's citizens would step back from the world, dedicating themselves solely to contemplation of the wonders of God.

After the lighting of the Sabbath candles, my brother and I walked down the moonlit street to synagogue. There were one hundred fifty of them in Monsey, he told me—one for every two hundred people in the community. Within a four-block radius of his house, he could choose from among the Viznitz shul, a 45,000-square-foot Romanesque structure that was one of the prides of the Hasidic world; the Vin synagogue, founded by a sect of Viennese Jews; a Sephardic basement temple frequented by Morrocans, Yemenis, and Israelis; a temple founded by the Litvisher scholars of Lithuania; and Bais Iyel, an informal, drop-in shul on Blauvelt Road that catered to all sects. Bais Iyel was my brother's everyday synagogue, he told me. He was close to its rabbi, and a regular user of its *mikvah*, a ritual purification bath that many observant Jews, but particularly Hasidim, take before the Sabbath.

A light snow had begun to fall, dusting the hedges and the maple trees along the quiet street. We passed clusters of bearded men wearing long black overcoats, some with large round beaver fur hats known as *streimels*. The guttural sounds of Yiddish carried through the air. Except for the cars parked in the driveways of the wood-shingle bungalows, we could have been walking through a nineteenth-century village in Poland. Bais Iyel occupied the basement of an old two-story house covered with white aluminum siding, located about three hundred yards down Blauvelt Road. Worshipers had begun assembling for the evening Sabbath prayer. My brother suggested we take a ritual bath beforehand.

The mikvah was located in a fluorescent-lit room in the

sub-basement, down a dingy flight of stairs. As we entered, we plucked crumpled white towels from bins by the door. Two skinny Hasidim were stripping silently, hanging their clothes from rusting hooks embedded in the blue tile wall.

A sign nailed to a concrete pillar provided a guide to mikvah etiquette:

> *Please do not leave wet towels on the floor of the mikvah.*
> *Don't you like a nice, clean mikvah?*
> *It's not nice to cause agmas nefesh to other people.*

Agmas nefesh, my brother explained, was spiritual distress.

At the back of the room, surrounded by a guardrail, two bathers were soaking in the holy pool: a sunken tub about the size of a health club Jacuzzi. The mikvah was a vital part of my brother's daily routine, but it was especially important before the Sabbath, he told me, as we began to take off our clothes. All of the *tumah*, the spiritual uncleanliness acquired by the soul during the weekdays, was washed away through immersion in water. A ritual immersion reestablished man's link with the Garden of Eden and returned him to a state of purity.

I gestured to a small pool beside the main tank. "What's that for?"

It was a receptacle for rainwater, my brother explained. According to Jewish law, the mikvah must consist of "a gathering" of natural water. The merging of the natural rainwater with the tap water was known as a *hashakah*—a kiss—and sanctified the water in the larger tank.

My brother peeled off layer after layer of clothing: black hat, skullcap, coat, vest, white shirt, undershirt, pants, jockey shorts, and finally, his talles, a white cotton shroud with seven knotted strings—*tsitsis*—dangling from its hem. It was the first time that I had seen my brother naked since we were children, and I was unsettled by his transformation. Deprived of physical exercise for years, his body had turned doughy and pot-bellied. He caught me looking at him and, with a self-conscious grin, reached behind his ears and uncoiled his peyyes. The side curls stuck out from his head like goat horns. For a moment my brother resembled an out-of-shape satyr or a paunchy Bacchus.

He tucked the side curls back behind his ears, showered in a grubby stall, and descended the three steps into the mikvah. I followed into the tepid chest-high water. My brother looked at me sharply and gestured to his wrist. My watch. I had forgotten his instructions: every external object must be stripped off the body or the soul cannot be thoroughly purified. He shut his eyes tightly and dunked himself several dozen times in rapid succession, drawing a short breath after each submersion. I watched him, mystified.

Minutes later, we dried ourselves, dressed, and climbed the stairs to the shul. We passed a sink at the top of the staircase.

"Wash your hands," he commanded.

"Wash? I just took a shower and a bath."

"Any time a Jew looks upon a naked body—even his own—he acquires a little bit of tumah. That has to be washed away." My brother spoke with such clear authority on this bit of Talmudic arcania that I was struck by the distance he had come from the thirteen-year-old boy who had struggled through his bar mitzvah readings. He had spent much of the last fifteen years, I knew, immersed in the study of the Talmud at a Monsey learning center, supporting himself and his family on a small stipend provided by wealthy Jewish contributors. My brother had transformed himself into a perambulatory encyclopedia of Jewish law and philosophy. He was what his community called a Talmud *chocher*—one of the highest callings to which an ultra-Orthodox Jew can aspire.

• • •

Ma'ariv, which was about to begin, was the last of the three daily prayers that my brother said in synagogue every day of his life. The synagogue itself had the informal feeling of a basement recreation room. Dirty gray linoleum tiles covered the floor, chipped away in places, exposing bare wooden planks. Along the left side of the fluorescent-lit space ran an eight-foot-high white screen, which sealed off the smaller women's section. The men stood or sat on hard-backed chairs behind six rows of wooden tables, divided into three sections. Dominating the center of the room was the *bimah*—a raised lectern surrounded by a metal guardrail, where the Torah reading took place. At the front of the room stood the Holy Ark, a three-paneled mahogany case inlaid with brass crowns and decorative gold Hebrew lettering. The center section contained the Torah, which was shielded from view by a blue velvet curtain embroidered with yellow roses. Rabbi Moshe Meisels, who ran the synagogue, sat beside the Ark. He was a bear-like man in his mid-forties, with a lustrous graying beard, a streimel, and a shiny black polyester jacket that strained around his ample middle. He took my hand in a vise-like grip.

"Shalom aleichem," he said. "So this is Tuvia's famous brother, visiting from California?"

"That's me," I said.

"Your first trip to Monsey?"

"First in a long while."

"You're welcome."

"He just had his first mikvah," said my brother.

Meisels's face lit up. "A mikvah?" he said. "Take a picture of him."

"A picture?"

"Take one of him now, and another a year from now, when he's wearing the streimel and peyyes, just so we can compare."

Everybody laughed.

Moshe Meisels, I learned, was the son of a distinguished rabbi from Hungary whose entire family had died in Auschwitz. After the war, Meisels's father had married another Hungarian survivor and moved to the south side of Chicago, where he founded the city's first Hasidic congregation, and where his son Moshe was born and raised. Moshe Meisels had opened Bais Iyel a decade ago, and his wife and thirteen children lived in the house above the shul.

My brother and I settled onto hard wooden seats as the prayers began. The worshipers were split evenly between Hasidim, identified by their extravagant fur hats, and non-Hasidic Jews, who wore more conservative black fedoras. All of the married men were draped in white, silver-brocaded prayer shawls. A handful of boys darted around the room. One climbed onto the platform and perched precariously on the metal guardrail, until his father jumped from his seat and yanked him back behind the prayer table.

As Meisels rose at the front of the room, the worshipers stood and faced the Ark. They began to chant, their lips gliding easily over the soft Hebrew syllables, a murmur building slowly into a rushing stream of prayer. The man behind me emitted a strange, high-pitched warble, and prostrated himself so that his forehead rested directly on the table in front of him, which was piled with Styrofoam coffee cups and tattered prayer books.

My brother began to daven. Eyes tight shut, right hand clutching his prayer book, he jerked up and down spasmodically, almost as if he was having a seizure. From deep within him rose a Hebrew wail that soared above the sixty other voices. Clenching his right hand into a fist, he punched the air with rapid-fire jabs. He pounded his fist against his chest and began to rotate his head, his mouth first slack jawed, then twisted into a grimace. The prayers seemed interminable. The wailing was interspersed with periods of quiet muttering. The worshipers sat, they stood,

they stepped back and forth. The prayer seemed to lack chore-
ography—each man immersed in his own dialogue. Finally, after
nearly an hour, my brother tilted his face heavenward and un-
leashed a climactic torrent of Hebrew. Then he sank onto the
wooden seat, his forehead glistening. I felt exhausted, a little
lost. Being surrounded by so many believers was a little like being
the only sober person at a party where everyone else was tripping
on acid.

"You were the most intense one there," I said as we stepped
out into the night.

"I'm a big davener."

I reminded him of the night in Jerusalem when he had
mocked the Hasidim davening in the old ultra-Orthodox quarter.

"You thought those people were crazy."

"They were crazy in love for Hashem."

"Those guys are your role models now?"

"Amazing, huh?" he said.

Ahuva had spent the afternoon and evening preparing the Sabbath meal. Like most ultra-Orthodox women, she attended synagogue only during holidays, or *yom tovs*, such as Rosh Hashanah,
Yom Kippur, and Passover, devoting her time to taking care of
her children, shopping, cleaning, and earning money for the family. My brother had worked sporadically during the thirteen years
of their marriage. Now he was unemployed again, and spent six
days a week studying Torah and Talmud. Aside from his small
stipend, the family lived off Ahuva's income from "Morah Hammer's Happy Home," a nursery school that she ran single-
handedly in the basement. She managed the school five days a
week—including a half day on Friday. As my brother and I returned from synagogue, she was sitting at the kitchen table, her

head in her hands, stealing a moment's peace before the next phase of the evening began.

At the table, a cacophony of voices blasted over me. Yankel showed off half-learned tricks with a yo-yo. Yosef Dov rattled off the starting lineup of the Yankees—an impressive feat, I thought, considering that his father believed baseball to be folly and banned television. Three-year-old Gnendi stared at me as if I'd beamed down from Mars; the baby, Dina Gittel, sobbed inconsolably. She was suffering from a urinary infection, Ahuva explained, as she patted her on the back, and they had been in and out of the hospital for the past two months. She walked around the table, trying to calm the baby, shouting in Yiddish at her noisy offspring.

The Sabbath meal unfolded as a series of finely honed rituals. First came the ceremonial washing: three alternating splashes of each hand, up to the wrist, with a two-handled plastic chalice. Then kiddush, the blessing over the wine. My brother filled a silver cup with wine until it was overflowing, sang in his thin, reedy voice, then drank the wine in three gulps. A few drops trickled down his chin and spilled on his collar, adding to the already formidable collection of wine and food stains that had turned his shirt into a Jackson Pollock canvas. Each member of the family, except the baby, drank a splash of the sweet liquid from a thimble-sized silver cup.

Next came *motzi*, the blessing over bread. My brother recited the prayer over two loaves of seeded challah, commemorating the extra portion of manna that the Israelites received on their first Sabbath in the Sinai desert. Then he tossed down chunks to everyone at the table. Blessings over, Ruchel and Ahuva brought out gefilte fish and salmon, vegetable soup, potato kugel, chicken legs, salad, tahini, hummus, tomato dip, and babaganush. Conversation swirled around me in Yiddish.

"You don't understand Yiddish?" asked Yankel, surprised.

"Dovid and Gnendi speak more Yiddish than English," my brother said approvingly.

When I had made my brief visit to Monsey before leaving for Africa, my brother's life had seemed inchoate. He and Ahuva had had only three children then; in my mind I had somehow believed that they were still capable of rejoining secular society. Now everything felt completely different. My brother was thirty-six, but he seemed decades older and deeply rooted, almost as if he had known no other life. As I had been roaming across continents, avoiding commitments, my brother had completed his transformation. He was the patriarch of a large and expanding clan of three sons and three daughters, and, evidently, a pillar of his community. Somehow, the younger brother whom I had disparaged as an unfocused drifter had metamorphosed into a respected Talmudic scholar, his knowledge of Judaic law and ritual as profound as that of many Monseyites twice his age. As I contemplated his evident success within the boundaries of his community, I was not sure whether to feel saddened by the person he had become or proud of his achievements, or somewhere in between.

As the meal drew to a close and the children cleared the table, he leaned forward and extended his hand.

"*L'chaim,*" he said. It meant, "to life."

I took his hand.

"*L'chaim,*" I replied.

THE LETTER DESCRIBING MY BROTHER'S EN-
try into the yeshiva was unsettling for all of us. Arriving
at my father's apartment on a Saturday morning in August
1981, it consisted of fifteen pages of breathless prose about
the decadence of the West, the tragedy of Jewish assimi-
lation, and the genius of great rabbis through the centuries.
The wisdom of the Torah, he wrote, was infinite: Judaism
was not just a religion, my brother enthused, but an all-
encompassing way of life. Jewish law governed how much
sleep a person got, when the best time for exercise was,
marriage, and divorce. Judaism did not deny the world, but
encouraged the pursuit of sensory pleasures. "On the most
spiritual of days, Shabbos, it is a commandment to eat
three full meals and highly suggested for a husband and
wife to have sexual relations."

My father and I looked at each other, eyebrows
raised. Tony had never mentioned the subject of sex before
in a family context.

"The aim in Judaism is not asceticism but control,"
he continued. "It is only through control over one's pas-

sions, using them for the highest goal—attaining a closer relationship with God—that one can find freedom."

I thought back to my brother's grubby Jerusalem apartment, his days and nights of pot smoking and aimless wandering. "Control" was not a word I had ever associated with him.

The journey of discovery had been joyous, he rhapsodized. "Being at a yeshiva and seeing people twenty, twenty-two years old, realizing there is meaning to life, and then seeing them shed their Western attitudes and lifestyle, is a tremendous experience. But even more so is to feel it happening to yourself."

Yet my brother said he had decided to return to America in November and enroll in Hobart College for the winter semester. "I don't feel that I am yet ready to make the change to religious life," he wrote. "At college I hope to keep some semblance of what I have learned here. I hope to take Hebrew as well as an independent course in Torah. I plan to keep Shabbos. But I know the going will be rough; the environment of Hobart is not exactly the best for a returning Jew. . . . If there is a great conflict between Hobart and Judaism, well, let me not think about that now. I pray only that I won't get swallowed up in American decadence and forget who I am, who my ancestors were, and the purpose we all have."

My father tossed the letter aside as we sat at the dining room table. It was eleven o'clock on a bright summer day, but the apartment, as usual, was shrouded in gloom. Weak light seeped in through two living room windows smudged by a decade's worth of urban grime. The dark blue and russet Persian carpet and thousands of old hardback books lining one wall seemed to absorb all the light in the room and accentuate the sense of murkiness. My father's pre-war Upper East Side apartment, with its hardwood floor, distinctive moldings, and high, beamed ceilings, had character, but I often felt claustrophobic here. The only direct sunlight shone—for about fifteen minutes a day—through a tiny window in a kitchen alcove that looked out over the East River and the Fifty-ninth Street Bridge.

"Do you know anything about this?"

"A little," I replied. I told him about my own stopover in the yeshiva. I recounted for him how Tony had warned me about the "brainwashing" tactics of the students and staff at Ohr Somayach, taken me on long walks in the hills above the holy city, and promised that he could refute any "proof" of God's existence that the professors there presented. I admitted that I had tried to nudge him toward spending a few days there, but that Tony had remained violently opposed to the idea. My brother had been the most resolute atheist I had known.

Partly because of that, both my father and I clung to the belief that this "conversion" of Tony's had no staying power. It was good for a couple of months perhaps, we reassured each other. My brother's attention span had proven notoriously short in the past, despite his initial fervor. Tony's dormant passions for the theater and politics would reawaken, we both maintained, once he returned to the United States.

A few weeks later, a box of clothes, books, and manuscripts arrived at the apartment C.O.D. from Jerusalem, along with a letter asking our father to forward the belongings to Hobart. Days after that, a travel agent in the West Forty-seventh Street diamond district called.

"Your son needs a plane ticket home," he said. The agent, a Hasidic Jew, insisted on selling my father a $1,200 round-trip fare.

"But why do I need a round-trip ticket?" our father protested.

"It's all that's available," the travel agent replied. "*Nu?* So you want that your son should be stranded?"

Our father guessed that the man was in cahoots with Ohr Somayach, and that the yeshiva was seeking to ensure that Tony would return to Jerusalem. Feeling helpless, he paid him the money. Twenty-four hours later, he drove to Kennedy Airport to meet Tony's flight. An Orthodox rabbi from Queens, a relative through marriage, had warned him to be prepared. "He won't be the same as when he left."

Tony stepped into the international arrivals wing at Kennedy looking dazed. He wore a winter parka, blue jeans, sneakers, a black nylon yarmulke and a scraggly beard. During the drive back into Manhattan, he seemed withdrawn and uncomfortable. Our father sensed he was in turmoil.

My brother moved back into the room he had lived in three years earlier. That first night back in New York City, he laid down the rules by which he would live: kosher food, separate plates for meat and dairy, and strict observance of the Sabbath. That Friday at sundown, he ushered in the Sabbath with candles and a kiddush, the prayer over wine, as our father and his wife, Arlene, looked on, then went out to visit his old circle of friends from Manhattan's High School of Performing Arts. Forbidden by Shabbos rules from carrying a key or ringing a doorbell, he sat on the stoop outside the locked door of the apartment building late that night for an hour, shivering in the late November chill, waiting for somebody to open it for him. Our father and Arlene, a former Broadway actress to whom he had been married for a decade, woke up to hear Tony stumbling around the apartment, trying to find his way to bed without turning on a light. Our father found the behavior baffling, disturbing. "It's madness," he told me.

I kept my distance physically and emotionally. I was living across town at the time, in a rundown studio apartment on the Upper West Side, writing articles about my Asian travels while searching for a staff writer job with a newspaper or magazine. The spiritual awakening I had briefly experienced in Jerusalem now felt like some drug-induced euphoria. Reading my journal, I winced at its earnest meditations on keeping kosher and attending synagogue. Perhaps my dalliance with ultra-Orthodox Judaism made me react more negatively to Tony's metamorphosis. When I saw my brother again at my father's apartment, wearing his tsitsis and yarmulke, I recoiled from him. His use of Hebrew phrases like "Baruch Hashem," his air of humorless certainty—none of it bore any resemblance to the goofy, hopelessly disorganized Tony I had known. In retrospect, I was perhaps not a little threatened by my brother's utter seriousness of purpose. No doubt the clownish, confused brother was more reassuring for me than the zealot he had suddenly become. It would wear off, I assured myself. I wouldn't argue with him. My brother seemed beyond arguments.

Friends in his theater clique from the High School of Performing Arts felt the same way. A half dozen of them met him at a coffee shop on Second Avenue in Manhattan a few days after his return. Rumors had been floating around the crowd that "something was up with Tony Hammer." Suddenly impervious to irony, Tony lectured them feverishly for a half hour on the truth of *yiddishkeit*—the Jewish way of life. He had, they recalled years later, the celestial fervor of an astronaut who had returned from a lunar landing.

"You have to see it," he said. "You must go and see it."

"What's gotten into you? Relax," one of his friends told him.

"You don't know what I've seen," he replied.

Some of them even thought it was a joke. My brother's friends were always putting each other on, and Tony's "Jewish routine" was the most convincing riff that any of them could remember. At the apartment on Ninety-second Street, they suppressed giggles as Tony ritualistically washed his hands with a plastic chalice in the kitchen sink. He said the blessing, then explained that a part of the Jewish soul, or *nashama*, resides in the fingertips and must be purified whenever one returns to the Jewish home from exposure to the spiritual pollution of the outside world. Tony—the debunker who was always asking, "Where's the scam? Who's scamming me?"—was putting one over on them, they assumed. But after several weeks they began to realize that it wasn't an act, and even his closest friends acknowledged: "We don't know how to talk to Tony Hammer anymore."

Concerned that he was starting to have second thoughts about his new course, the Jerusalem yeshiva sent emissaries from its sister school in Monsey, New York, to encourage him to stand firm in his faith. One morning two young men wearing identical black fedoras, suits, and beards—the look I recalled from Ohr Somayach—rang the doorbell and entered our father's apartment with an awkward greeting. They stood in the dining area beside the front door, arms folded, expressionless, waiting wordlessly until my brother finished dressing and went out the door with them. Our father encountered the pair the next day sitting on a carved marble bench in the building's austere lobby. He nodded a stiff greeting, and they ignored him. They became an inescapable presence, lurking around the building so often that the elevator man complained about them. Our father called them "the creeps." They would telephone—three, four times a day—querying anyone who answered. The few times I talked to them, I was unhelpful, without being entirely rude.

"Hello, Tony?"

"He's out."

"So, where is he?"

"I don't know."

"And how long has he been away?"

"I have no idea."

"So, when will he be there?"

"Sometime this evening, I guess."

"What's he doing?"

"I have no idea."

"Fine, then, I'll call again."

We knew that my brother was torn. He was spending much of his time with the Squat Theater Company, an improvisational troupe in Greenwich Village that he had studied with during his sophomore year at Hobart. He was drifting between worlds, drawn back to fragments of his former life: his acting guru, Stanislavsky; his literary idol, Bertolt Brecht; the Metropolitan Museum of Art; Chick Corea; marijuana. Then, in the late fall, he returned to Hobart College for a visit, preparing himself, we thought, for his reenrollment in January. The dean at Hobart had assured him that the college would provide him with a single room and kosher cuisine.

But my brother returned from the long weekend trip subdued. Shortly before Chanukah, the yeshiva "creeps" came back to my father's apartment and invited Tony to join them for a weekend visit to Ohr Somayach. "Some of your friends from Israel are up in Monsey for the holidays," one of them said. "They've been asking about you."

They rode the Monsey Trails bus together on a Thursday afternoon. Tony would never really come home again.

And then, as if seized by a dybbuk, he was no longer Tony. "My name is Tuvia," he declared a few months later, after showing up at our father's house without notice from the yeshiva in Monsey, carrying a paper bag filled with kosher food and his own plates and silverware. His beard was fuller, his tone more strident, his attitude more critical of the secular life he had discarded. He had delayed his reenrollment at Hobart—indefinitely. I could sense a steely new resolve.

The ensuing encounters—at least once a month, during Sunday visits on his weekly day off from Ohr Somayach and later, a second yeshiva called Kol Yakov—were charged with acrimony. Neither our father nor I considered simply accepting Tony's choice. We saw it as our mission to shake him out of it. He was throwing his life away, we both told him, abandoning his promise for a world of meaningless ritual and superstition. Once again I had ganged up with our father against Tony, drawing encouragement from his overt hostility to my brother. He was furious about Tony's apparent conviction that none of his secular obligations mattered anymore. One day he confronted him in the hallway, waving a letter he had received from Hobart College's financial aid office. He asked Tony when he planned to repay the thousand-dollar loan and the plane ticket to Israel that he had received from Hobart.

"I'm discussing it with the rabbis," my brother replied evasively, heading for the kitchen. "They're advising me what to do."

"Are they advising you to pay it back?"

"They're dealing with it."

"Are you ever planning to go back to college?"

"I'm learning every day," he replied.

His eyes lit up as he began to tell us about the eleventh-century French rabbinical scholar Rashi, the Egyptian Jew Moses Maimonides, known as the Rambam, the Lithuanian scholar known as the Vilna Gaon, the early twentieth-century Litvisher rabbi Chafitz Chaim. They were, he said, "the greatest men in the history of civilization."

Our father looked pained. "Shakespeare? Mozart? Winston Churchill? They don't count?"

"Like insects compared to the *tsaddikim*."

"How are you planning to earn a living?" our father demanded.

"Don't worry," he said with a shrug. "It will take care of itself."

Tony washed his hands, ritually, in the kitchen sink, using a plastic two-handled vessel he had brought with him, along with his kosher lunch, from Monsey. Then he threw himself down on a couch in the living room, thumbed through the magazines he used to devour—*The New Yorker, The New York Review of Books, The Atlantic*—and made an ostentatious display of tossing them aside. Pacing back and forth in front of my father's bookshelves, Tony ran his fingers at random across the H section, past the works of Thomas Hardy, Bret Harte, Joseph Heller, Ernest Hemingway. What was the use of all these books? he said. The Chumash, the five books of Moses, he declared, and the Oral Torah, the Talmud, were all a person needed to live a full, moral life.

"God gave Moses the entire Torah?" I asked.

"No question."

"He handed him a scroll with the whole future of the Israelites set in writing?"

"One hundred percent."

I was in his face now. "All right, how old is the world?"

"It says in the Torah. Hashem created it five thousand seven hundred and forty-four years ago."

"What about the scientific data? Geological strata? Fossils?"

"Hashem deliberately put the fossils there to test man's faith."

Our father, who had been listening to our argument silently, now shook his head in disbelief. "My God," he said. "Three years ago you were doing that monologue from *Inherit the Wind* in acting class. Defending Darwin."

My brother whirled around. "Well, I know differently now. Look at the human body," he said. "Think of the power of your brain, your lungs, your heart pumping oxygen through your body. Expand that to the entire cosmos. Did all that just happen by itself? How can you stand there and tell me that God doesn't exist?"

"He may exist, in some form," I interrupted. "But how does it follow that God singled out the Jewish people for special treatment?"

"We know it's a fact." He began to pace again, eyes boring into us like lasers. "The Torah tells us that two million people—two million—received direct communication from the Almighty on Mount Sinai. Those two million then told their children, who told their grandchildren, on through the generations. In every other religion some goy went into a cave and saw the light. He came back and told his followers, and a few centuries later they had a religion. But for Judaism to be false, you would have to say that every single one of those two million people were liars."

I followed him across the room. "Or you'd have to say that the Torah wasn't given to man by God, but was written by man."

"You don't want to accept it," he said. "Because if you did accept it, you would have to change your life around completely. And that's difficult. Believe me, I know. Our *taivas* are very strong."

"Our *taivas*?"

"Earthly desires."

I was astonished at how completely and unskeptically my brother had taken on every strand of Orthodoxy. I decided to play my ace in the hole.

"The Holocaust doesn't shake your faith, then?"

My brother remained unfazed. He had an answer for that too.

"Not at all. We think of the Holocaust as a weeding-out process. A punishment for the spiritually dilapidated state of the Jews."

"What? The Polish Jews were the most religious Jews in the world. But they suffered the most of anyone."

"There are a lot of theories about that," he said. "There's an idea in the Torah that if one Jew strayed from the path, the Lord decreed that thirty-five would suffer. God was in the gas chambers telling the Jews, 'This is what happens when you turn your back on me. This is what happens when you allow man to control the world.' "

"So the Holocaust was the fault of the Jews, not Hitler?"

"Hitler is burning in hell, but he did the Jews a favor. A lot of these Jews were people who would have been cut off from the world to come, but they died because they were Jews. Those who were killed for being Jews are in a much higher place than even kaddish—the prayer for the dead—can reach."

"Tony, your arguments make no sense." I sank down on the couch, light-headed.

My brother's views on every subject seemed to have been permeated by his conversion. There was a new intolerance, a fiercely moralizing tone that stood in striking contrast to his previous open-mindedness. The AIDS virus, which was beginning to cut a swath through the country's homosexual population, was the revenge of the Almighty against the *to'evahs*—the impure ones—for their violation of the Torah, he declared. "The universe is a big mechanism," he would say. "Think of it as a giant assembly plant. One screw put in upside down can have grave consequences. A car roof might be screwed in wrong, and the whole vehicle could collapse. Why do you think certain types of monkeys were eliminated from Noah's Ark?" he asked. "Because these animals had imitated certain human behavior, and God decreed that they had to be left behind."

Homosexuals weren't the only objects of his disdain. All Arabs, he said, were "terrorists."

"But I was with you in Israel," I reminded him. "I seem to recall your spending a lot of time in the Arab Quarter. What was that about?"

"You don't understand," he said.

Of course it wasn't going to last, our father reassured himself, after Tony had boarded the bus back to Monsey. His son, the graduate of High School of Performing Arts, the star of *Equus* and *The Man Who Came to Dinner*, was trying out another part: "Tony's ultimate character work," he called it. Sooner or later he'd grow tired of the role, as he always did.

Our mother, now living with her companion in North Carolina, refused to criticize her son. If my brother wanted to devote his life to Judaism, she said, that was his decision. There were far worse choices that he could make. "We should consider ourselves lucky," she said. "He could be taking drugs. He could be wearing saffron robes, chanting Hare Krishna, and banging a drum on Times Square."

"I don't see the difference," I told her.

"Of course there's a difference. The Jewish people go back five thousand years. It's an ethical system. It's a family way of life."

"They're as brainwashed as the Moonies," I snapped. As far as I was concerned, Tony's personality had been deleted by a sinister cabal of rabbis: they had seized him in a moment of weakness and indoctrinated him with religious mumbo-jumbo. I was furious at these sect leaders for what they did to him, but even more, I was ashamed of my brother, did not want to be associated with him, did not want what I saw as his "weak character" to be tied to me in any way. It was another Hammer family embarrassment to conceal, like the divorce of our parents fourteen years earlier.

"Why can't you just accept him?" our mother asked.

"I can't accept him like this," I replied.

It was not merely the loss of his sense of humor, of irony, I told myself. It was not only the fact that every time we got together I was forced to endure his lectures on the glorious afterlife that awaited the believers, the untrustworthiness of "the other nations" of the world—a code for the gentiles. It was not merely that he seemed to look upon his family as lost souls. It was also that my brother reminded me acutely of my own failures. The letter he had written upon his arrival in the holy land—"Israel has been a father, a brother, a mother to me"— echoed through my mind. Was there a hidden rebuke in that remark? I wondered. And perhaps there were aspects of Tony's ultra-Orthodoxy that made me uncomfortable about my life. I had just been hired as a staff writer for *People* magazine, and though I was delighted to have the job, the contrast between my brother's world and mine could hardly have been starker. Tony's sharply defined identity stood against my own lack of clarity, the suspicion that my chosen profession was a shallow one.

I continued to hope that it would end, that he would show up at the door one afternoon and announce that it had all been a mistake, he had left Ohr Somayach and was going back to Hobart. But after nearly two years in Monsey, when my brother turned twenty-three, he telephoned our mother and told her that he was engaged to be married. Ahuva was a yeshiva student in Monsey. She had grown up in Queens and been raised as an Episcopalian before finding her way back, *baruch Hashem*, to her Jewish roots. Three weeks later, the invitations were sent out. They announced—in Hebrew and English—the nuptials of "T. Hammer and A. Bachmann" on Sunday, the nineteenth of August, 1984, or the nineteenth day of Av in the Jewish year 5744.

I STARED AT THE WEDDING INVITATION IN the dark stairwell of my apartment building, feeling nauseous and dizzy. It was the realization, I thought, of my worst fears. I saw my brother's engagement as the final step in a diabolical plan concocted by Monsey's rabbis to lure him into the fold for life. I conjured up a bleak vision of my brother's future: a dozen children in a hovel in Rockland County, days spent burrowed in an airless reading room in some ultra-Orthodox shul, a life of destitution and archaic rituals and total estrangement from his family. I phoned our father that afternoon.

"They've got him," I said. "They've fucking got him."

"Not necessarily," he replied. "We don't know anything about this girl. Maybe she'll drag him out of there."

"We could hire a deprogrammer," I said halfheartedly. I knew it was a fantasy, but the notion of forcibly wresting Tony from the community had a certain last-ditch appeal. I wanted my brother back, and if the rabbis were rushing him into a marriage to someone I assumed he barely knew, no counterstrategy seemed too extreme. One week locked into a motel room on the New Jersey Turnpike could still bring Tony to his senses, I thought.

"That's ridiculous," our father barked.

I turned on him. "Why did you ever allow those guys from the yeshiva into the apartment? Why didn't you tell them to get lost?"

"It was Tony's apartment too," he said. Our father's response angered me. You spineless bastard, I found myself thinking. You could have stopped them. But I said nothing.

The timing of my brother's wedding could not have been worse for our family. For years my father had been dogged by lawsuits from alleged Mafia figures who claimed they had been libeled in his book about the Italian American crime boss Lucky Luciano and in a series of magazine articles about organized crime. Now there was a new calamity. A tax shelter that had harbored his earnings from the Luciano project had just been ruled illegal, and—on top of everything else—he was being hit with a decade's worth of back taxes, plus interest and penalties. As the wedding plans went forward, tax collectors raided bank accounts, seized his Buick Skylark from the street, and auctioned it off for a few thousand dollars. Weeks before the wedding, Arlene telephoned me at the office. In her voice I caught a quaver that I had never heard before.

"What's wrong?"

"It's terrible," she said. "They're putting us out on the street."

A housing court judge had ordered them to pay nearly a year's back rent or face immediate eviction. Our family closed ranks. Arlene's parents, my father's cousin, and I pooled our resources to rescue them. The threat of homelessness receded. But they had come within days of losing their apartment, and the experience was terrifying. My family seemed to be losing its moorings. And now my brother was getting married.

Tony brought Ahuva down from Monsey by bus to meet our father and Arlene at their apartment weeks before their marriage. Ahuva was charming, if a little smug, Arlene reported back to me—talked about her starring role in *Arsenic and Old Lace* in high school, joked that the best part about being ultra-Orthodox was never having to shop for a bathing suit again. Arlene chatted with her about her own acting career—she was starring in a trio of one-act plays on Roosevelt Island—and came away with a sense, she recalls, that Ahuva was far more grounded than my brother, more attached to the secular world, and that she might one day lead my brother out of Monsey.

At four-thirty on a humid August afternoon, we climbed into a rented Ford sedan and set out on the drive to Rockland County. The mood in the car was somber. Arlene had tucked her shoulder-length auburn hair beneath a short red wig, a prop from her role years before in a production of Carson McCullers's *Member of the Wedding*. She wore a long-sleeved green blouse and green skirt that reached her ankles. Emily, my five-year-old half sister, sat beside her. My father squirmed in a tight blue blazer and gray pants. My grandmother Mildred sat in the front seat, despondent.

"I still don't understand why you have to wear that wig," she told Arlene, sounding like a clichéd version of the fretting Jewish grandmother. "You have beautiful hair."

"Mother, give it a rest," said my father.

"Moe always had such high hopes for him," she muttered. My grandfather had died four years earlier.

The day was hot, muggy, oppressive. We pulled into the crowded parking lot of the Spring Valley Yeshiva, a two-story white-brick edifice set back from Monsey's main intersection. My father and I both slipped on black nylon yarmulkes before stepping out of the car. Relatives from both sides of my family milled awkwardly around the parking lot and the manicured lawn beside the yeshiva building—not certain, it seemed to me, how to approach this occasion. My mother, cloaked in a shapeless gray smock, with a yellow linen scarf covering her hair and dangling halfway down her back, had turned herself into a reasonable facsimile of a Yiddisher mama. But her effort was offset by the appearance nearby of her best friend June, an eccentric widowed playwright who lived alone in a tenement on the Upper West Side of Manhattan. Today, June was a frightening apparition. Her pasty white face, bright red lip gloss, bobbed orange hair, and black-on-white polka dotted minidress all suggested an aging flapper.

"Why did you bring her here?" I demanded.

My mother looked surprised. "She's known you and Tony since you were children."

"She looks ridiculous."

My mother began to walk away from me. "Try to smile," she said over her shoulder. "Try to respect your brother. Today is his day."

Without a word I turned toward the yeshiva, not really knowing where I was going, nodding at relatives and staring down clusters of ultra-Orthodox men and women. I was overwhelmed, close to tears. I could not wrap my mind around the fact that my brother was going through with the wedding; the reality of his religious metamorphosis now seemed inescapable, immutable. A half dozen religious guests, talking together in a semicircle on the lawn—yeshiva scholars and married men—stopped their conversation and smiled at me.

"How are you?" a stout middle-aged man wearing a gray beard asked. It was all the provocation that I needed.

"How am I? I'm not good," I blurted. "That's my brother you people are marrying off today."

He shifted about uneasily. "You have a problem with that?"

"I have a big problem with that."

"What are you yelling for?" he asked. "Be calm."

I glared at the man. "What gives you the right to take people from their families?"

"Nobody took him from anybody's family. There's no need to get so excited."

My face was inches from his. "You've turned him into a zombie."

I turned and walked away, my heart racing. Moments later, I saw my brother greeting guests gathering at the entrance to the yeshiva building. Tony seemed elated.

"Hellooo," he said, drawing out the final syllable in a way I had never heard him do before. His voice had taken on a deeper timbre in the few months since I had last seen him. "I'm glad you could come."

"How could I miss . . . this?" I said, managing a weak smile as I shook his hand.

"So, you're excited?"

"How could I not be? Fulfilling the mitzvah of marriage is one of the joys of being a Jew."

What was left to say? I looked into his eyes and could find nothing familiar there. "Congratulations," I said.

At six thirty, the two hundred guests filed toward the *chupah*—the cloth wedding canopy, hung from four wooden posts, that symbolizes the home that unites bride and groom. The canopy had been erected on the front lawn of the yeshiva, in view of a stream of traffic. My father, stepmother, grandmother, and I found ourselves stuck at the periphery of the crowd of strangers—symbolic, I thought, of our marginal place within my brother's new ultra-Orthodox community. A roiling sea of black coats and fedoras separated us from the chupah. My half sister

Emily perched on my father's shoulders. Near us Ahuva's family gathered, minus her father, who, we would later discover, had cut off all contact with his daughter following her engagement. Beneath the chupah, fifty yards away, my brother davened feverishly, flanked by a cluster of rabbis. Cloaked in a black overcoat on top of his white marriage gown, Tony bobbed up and down robotically. Stooped, bearded, he seemed ageless—thirty, forty, sixty, it was impossible to tell. He looked, I said to my father, like a troll in a trance. Our grandmother, who had not seen my brother since he had entered the yeshiva three years earlier, peered at the bearded figure in the distance.

"Dick," she said, "Who is that?"

"That's Tony—your grandson."

She looked stricken. "No. It can't be. My God, Dick. He looks like an old man."

Suddenly, a hush fell over the crowd as the bride made her entrance. Two young women led Ahuva by the arm to the chupah. She shuffled forward, nearly tripping over the heavy antique bridal gown that billowed around her. An opaque white veil concealed her face. She turned toward my brother and circled him slowly seven times. The rabbi chanted the first wedding blessing, the Hebrew verses barely audible from where we stood. My brother slipped a gold ring on his bride's finger, and then other black-coated rabbis gathered in a semicircle and took turns reading the marriage contract and seven blessings. Tony and Ahuva sipped wine from a silver cup. Then, with an exuberant stomp, my newly married brother shattered a wineglass encased in a blue velvet sleeve.

"Mazel tov!" yelled the crowd in unison. And so it was done. Our father stared straight ahead, expressionless. Tony and his bride strode down the aisle, surrounded by well wishers, and disappeared into a bedroom for a custom that had been coyly explained on the invitation: "After they walk out from the chupah, the kallah (bride) and the chusan (groom) are led to a private room which they enter alone. This private meeting now completes the wedding ceremony, and the couple are now man and wife in all respects."

The rabbis ushered my family back up the path to the reception hall, where the marriage feast was about to begin. In a stark room with scuffed white walls and fluorescent track lighting along the high ceilings, two dozen round tables had been set with white tablecloths, Styrofoam cups, paper plates, plastic knives and forks, plastic liter-sized bottles of kosher cola, and bottles of sweet wine. I ran my hands over a blue felt curtain that divided the men from the women. My father fidgeted beside me, glancing toward a crack in the curtain, trying to make eye contact with Arlene.

Young Hasidic waiters carried out the courses one by one: gefilte fish, oily salmon, challah bread, rubbery chicken legs and cholent, a thick, pasty stew of beans, potatoes, and beef. As I started to eat, the oil from the salmon seeped through the paper plate and onto the white tablecloth. An old man with a ragged gray beard and a threadbare suit came by the table and shook a fist filled with coins in my face. His fingernails were dirty, I noticed, and his suit was stained with oil from the fish.

"Nu?" he said. "Far der Chevra Kadisha?"

"What?" I said sharply.

"Chevra Kadisha," he repeated. "Give something to the Jewish burial society."

"No," I said.

Thirty minutes into the meal, Tony suddenly burst through the doorway, back from his encounter with his bride. We watched, bewildered, as a gaggle of young black-clad men and teenagers leapt out of their chairs and hoisted him in an armless wooden chair. A sprightly Yiddish song crackled from a speaker. The chair dipped and rocked precariously, threatening to send Tony—who was beaming with joy—plunging to the floor.

"Mazel tov, chusan," they cried. Good luck, bridegroom.

As the older ultra-Orthodox men watched quietly from the tables, sipping wine and amaretto, the young men grew increasingly animated. They whirled around my brother in a tight circle, clapping their hands above their heads. A half dozen then broke free of the circle. Squatting side by side, the six men kicked their legs out in a vigorous Russian-style peasant dance. As the men continued their dance, their comrades thrust the chair holding my brother higher, clapping, singing, and whirling around him. Women peeked from behind the curtain as Tony, with a cry of fear and euphoria, suddenly toppled backward into the arms of the crowd. Our father and I watched the spectacle silently, stiffly, feeling more like outsiders than ever. Tony brushed past us, not even making eye contact, and sat down at the center table, flanked by a duo of rabbis. The message from the crowd seemed clear, I thought. We were not welcome here.

As the meal drew to a close, the guests and hangers on began to drift away. A young Hasid passed our table and eyed somebody's abandoned half-finished dinner. Wordlessly, he snatched the plate, drew it up close to his lips, and, with a plastic spoon, shoveled the leftovers, a runny stew of salmon skin, chicken bones, horseradish, and challah crumbs, into his mouth. He moved to the next plate and slurped the remains off that as well.

"Good God," my father said, turning away. I was equally disgusted. I wanted to escape from this prison. I needed air. I would not wait for the cutting of the wedding cake.

"I'm out of here," I told my father. Waving a feeble farewell, I got up and bolted for the parking lot.

My brother and Ahuva honeymooned in a Catskills bungalow, moved into a small basement apartment in the oldest neighborhood in Monsey, and began new lives as husband and wife. He was going to spend his life, he told our father, studying the Talmud—not to become a rabbi, which he considered beyond his abilities, but to become a "better Jew."

So while other ultra-Orthodox Jews commuted into midtown Manhattan from their suburban enclave to sell insurance or diamonds or discount cameras, Tony spent his days cloistered in a *kollel*, a yeshiva for married men. The stipend, provided by wealthy Jewish donors, was about three hundred dollars a month. My brother earned a little pocket money working for an ultra-Orthodox wholesaler of musical instrument parts—packing violin strings, trumpet valves, and clarinet reeds into boxes for an hour a day. Ahuva taught at a kindergarten for Orthodox Jewish children. Our mother, as always, took a positive view of my brother's life. Tony was learning administrative skills, she told me, he was gaining responsibility, he was valued by his boss. But to me it seemed as if he were frittering away his early promise in menial labor, and I began to shut him further out of my life.

One afternoon in the fall, as I sat behind my cluttered desk at *People*, the security guard in the lobby phoned me to tell me I had visitors. "Mr. and Mrs. Hammer here to see you," he said.

"Mr. and Mrs. Hammer?"

Then I guessed: Tony and Ahuva.

I froze at my desk, seized by panic. Quite simply, I was terrified by the prospect of receiving them in my office. None of my colleagues—not even my close friends—knew much about my younger brother. I had never mentioned to anyone at the office that I had recently attended his wedding. In my anger and disappointment, I had come to view Tony as a shameful secret that had to be concealed. I did not want my colleagues whispering about him in the hallways, speculating about what had caused my brother to retreat into his blissed-out, brainwashed state.

Three minutes later, they appeared in the doorway. My brother, with his fedora, suit, and Mephistophelian beard. Ahuva, a plump, doe-eyed teenager wearing a long black dress with a white collar and a bulky mane of artificial hair. They looked like time travelers—shtetl dwellers in the plush hallways of the Time-Life Building.

"Hello, big brother," he said. "We were in the neighborhood."

"What a surprise," I said, squirming in my chair.

Tony and Ahuva took a few tentative steps into the huge office. They took in the plush couches, glass coffee tables, thirty-foot-long bank of windows overlooking Fifty-first Street. A departing senior editor had just vacated it, and it was absurdly luxurious for somebody so low on the corporate totem pole.

"Wow," he said. "Very nice."

"It's temporary."

"Still, they must like you, huh?"

"No real problems so far."

"Baruch Hashem."

"So . . . What brings you to Sodom?"

"We were visiting a rabbi in Brooklyn. Now we're on our way back to Monsey."

"Married life suiting you?"

"A *geshmakh* experience."

"A what?"

"*Geshmakh*. Delightful."

They stood there for a moment, silent. Then Tony asked: "Can we sit down?"

"Why not?" I gestured.

They took seats on the couch against the wall, facing my desk. Ahuva clasped her hands primly in her lap. She looked at me with an uncomfortable smile. I had met my sister-in-law just once before the wedding, an awkward encounter at my father's apartment. We had said little at the time. She must have known how I felt about my brother's religious life, and my body language made it clear that I didn't welcome her arrival into the family. Tony glanced over the detritus of my career: press passes hanging from a bulletin board, large framed black-and-white photographs of me and various eminences I had interviewed: Saul Bellow, Nadine Gordimer, the teenage actress Phoebe Cates.

"So . . . what are you working on?"

"The same old stuff," I said with a shrug. "Personality journalism at its finest."

"I'm sure a lot of people would love to have your job." My brother often asked our mother how much money I made, what kind of pieces I'd been writing, how soon I'd be promoted up the masthead. I took it as a hopeful sign: perhaps the secular world hadn't totally relinquished its hold on him, I thought.

But Tony hadn't come up here to make small talk. He was seeking a reconciliation. He did not want us to end up having the same rancorous relationship that he had with our father, he told me, unable to talk without bellowing in each other's faces. He hoped that I would welcome Ahuva into our family and no longer "be a stranger." The apartment on Hopal Lane was tiny, but they would always make room for me, he said.

"You should visit for Shabbos. Spend the weekend."

"One of these days," I said, certain that I would never set foot again in Monsey. I cast a nervous glance into the corridor.

"We're not just saying that," Ahuva said. "We really mean it."

A figure appeared at the doorway. It was my closest friend at the magazine, a talented writer from Long Island, known for his irreverent wit. He gazed with curiosity at the figures on the couch.

'Hey," I stammered. "Uhhh, this is my brother and . . . his wife."

"Humph," my friend said, surprised. "I didn't know you had a brother."

My friend shook my brother's hand, then reached for Ahuva's as well. She shrank back. An Orthodox Jewish married woman is forbidden to touch any man but her husband. I winced.

"They were just heading out," I said, turning to my brother and his wife. "I'll walk you to the elevator." Relief washed over me as the elevator doors closed behind them.

If I sometimes felt that my attitude toward my brother was unreasonable, that I was being judgmental, unduly harsh, all I had to do was look to our father for validation. He never accepted Ahuva, and his bitterness toward my brother seemed to grow after the wedding. Like me, he refused to call him by the name he had adopted—Tuvia. We would joke about Tony's marriage to Ahuva—"a Hoover, the vacuum cleaner"—and his pattern of dependency on stronger women. "He's always needed a mommy," our father said.

He would muse aloud about my brother's bizarre political odyssey. As a lifetime liberal Democrat, he had watched his son metamorphose from Democrat to Marxist Leninist through his latest incarnation, Reaganite conservative. "Tony doesn't even think for himself anymore," he lamented. "He just votes the way the rabbis tell him to vote."

But the episode that provoked him most began with a phone call he received from Tony about our parents' long-dissolved marriage.

"I'd like you to get a *get* from mom." Tony demanded. The word was Hebrew, meaning a Jewish divorce.

"A *get*? Why should I get a *get*?"

Our father's divorce from our mother in a civil procedure in Tijuana, Mexico, in the summer of 1970 was not recognized under Orthodox Jewish law, Tony said. That meant that our mother could never marry her companion, Mitchell, and that our father's remarriage to Arlene was invalid. Tony had it all arranged: all our father had to do was to appear before a *beis din*—the Jewish high court of law, consisting of three rabbis—at an ultra-Orthodox synagogue he had picked out in Brooklyn and receive the bill of divorce. He was to sign a Hebrew document before two witnesses stating that he was releasing our mother from her marriage vows. Then the document—containing the expression "I am sending you away"—was to be delivered to her, either in person or through a representative of our father.

"Please, would you just think about it?" Tony asked.

"I'll think about it," our father said grudgingly.

A half hour later he called Tony back.

"I've thought about it," he said.

"And you'll do it?"

"Under no conditions whatsoever. Your mother and I had a Reform marriage. And according to you people, that doesn't count, right?"

"Under *halacha*—Jewish law—no."

"So why do I need a get?"

"It would be better for all concerned."

"But, according to you, my marriage to your mother wasn't legal to begin with, right?"

"Technically not."

"So what does that make you?"

Tony never brought up the subject again.

It became even easier to distance myself from my brother as he began to cast off friends and relatives, one by one. The first to be shunted aside were Arlene's parents, Norman and Martha Nadel, who had treated us as their own grandchildren from the day we met them in 1970—sailing with us in the Atlantic Ocean, taking us to the theater. But Martha was a gentile, a churchgoing Methodist, and, in Tony's eyes, Norman had committed one of the gravest sins a Jew can commit, marrying outside the faith. The Nadels sent wedding presents, letters, birthday cards. My brother never acknowledged them. Norman told Martha to stop.

"They hate you," he said. "You're being treated as nothing because you're not Jewish."

"It doesn't matter how it's received," Martha said.

Tony set his sights on Arlene next. She was Martha's daughter, half Methodist, a gentile according to the Torah. Thus the woman who had encouraged his acting talent, who had spent countless hours rehearsing scenes with him and discussing the plays of Shakespeare, Arthur Miller, Clifford Odets, and who had comforted him through a series of tragedies in his teenage years, was now regarded with indifference, even suspicion. Eventually he would not be alone in the same room with her. If she handed him a piece of fruit, he would wash it ostentatiously before eating it.

Our father watched my brother's behavior with mounting fury. Finally, he wrote Tony a letter accusing him of spurning "all the people who believed in you." Back came a letter from my brother, filled with quotations from the Torah, tsaddikim, even the rabbis in his community, all justifying his belief that marriage to a non-Jew was a sin in the eyes of God, and would lead, ultimately, to the destruction of the Jewish people. He could make no exceptions, he wrote, even in the case of his stepmother.

"The goyim are here for a different purpose," he lectured me during a brief encounter outside the Metropolitan Museum of Art one summer afternoon. "Certain nations, such as the Dutch, are special. But the Jews' whole argument is that inside every goy is an Adolf Hitler. There's hatred for the Jews deep down."

I was aghast. Again, I found myself astonished by the totality of his indoctrination, by his unquestioning embrace of such harsh intolerance. "You would really lump your own stepmother and her mother in that group?"

"Individually perhaps not, but there is a mass thinking that goes on when they all get together."

Tony and Ahuva's first child was born on New Year's Day, 1986, a girl named Ruchel Basia. They named her after Ahuva's Jewish great-great-grandmother and Pharaoh's daughter who had rescued Moses from the bullrushes and later converted to Judaism. Our mother and Mitchell visited Ahuva in the hospital. Our father dutifully made the trip to Monsey, along with Arlene, to visit his first grandchild. I did not even send a card. A second child arrived in October 1987, a son named Yosef Dov. Again, the grandparents drove to Monsey, and again I refused to go along.

While my brother's family grew, my own life followed a meandering course. I left *People* magazine, became a freelance magazine writer in New York, traveled on frequent assignments overseas, spent an aimless year in Los Angeles, then returned to New York and a job as a writer for *Newsweek*. Throughout this period my encounters with my brother took place once, maybe twice a year—always at our father's apartment. The reunions were tense, awkward. The lack of outdoor activity and the diet of heavy Jewish food had begun to take a toll on my brother: in contrast to the lean, physically fit young man who had stood naked on a college stage in *Equus* nearly a decade earlier, he had begun to look pudgy and pasty. His eyes weakened, and he now wore thick-lensed, metal-framed glasses. He had let his beard grow out, obeying to the letter a Talmudic prohibition against cutting facial hair.

"Don't you ever get any exercise, Tony?" our father asked during one Sunday visit.

Tony shrugged. "I've got more important things to do."

Tony and his wife sat down at the dining room table, said blessings over the challah and whitefish they brought with them in plastic containers. Then the arguments began. There had just been a high-profile killing in New York. A young African American from the Harlem projects, a promising scholarship student at Exeter Academy, had attempted to mug an off-duty police officer near Central Park and been shot dead. The tragedy, the young man's double life, seemed to be on every New Yorker's mind that week.

My brother shrugged. "What do you expect from the *schvartzes?*"

"For God's sake," our father said, reddening. "One of your two best friends was black. Or have you forgotten him?"

Tony said nothing.

Old photograph albums were brought out, and as the family gathered around them, we talked about Allison, our half sister who had died almost exactly ten years earlier, at the age of two and a half. Allison's death had caused our father and Arlene intense anguish, and though the birth of their second daughter, Emily, had brought them consolation, they had never fully recovered from her loss. Her death had wounded me as well, but my brother had been even more deeply affected by it. Today, though, he showed no sign of lingering grief.

"It's too bad you don't believe the way we do, because then you could accept it," he told our father and Arlene. "It would help you to understand."

"So her death is now acceptable to you?" our father asked.

"I understand there are reasons for all things," he said. "But only Hashem knows exactly what those reasons are."

The mood of the reunion deteriorated further. "Tony," our father asked him, "what was so wonderful about the nineteenth century that you feel compelled to go and relive it? You want to live in a world of pogroms and shtetls? That was such a great time? What happens when the Messiah comes?" he asked. "Are you all going to get a first-class one-way ticket on the magic carpet? There's not going to be much room left in Israel for all those Jews."

After the birth of their third son, Dovid—named after our Talmudic scholar great-great grandfather—Tony and Ahuva stopped coming to Manhattan. They would not expose their children to Sodom, my brother explained. Our father, Arlene, and Emily continued to trek to Monsey once, sometimes twice a year. Our father refused to wear a yarmulke. He would play catch in the small front yard with his two oldest grandsons as Tony stood by in his dark suit, watching nervously. Although

Ahuva seemed more relaxed about exposing the boys to sports, she too was sensitive to the threat of secular contamination. When Emily was about twelve years old, she told Ruchel that she wanted to become a ballet dancer.

"What's ballet?" asked Ruchel, then five.

Ahuva cut Emily off before she could answer. Later, Arlene sent the family a photograph of Emily performing in her tutu at the neighborhood Jewish center. Ahuva placed the picture in a drawer, out of sight of her children. "I don't really feel sorry for Tony," our father told me after that incident. "He's made his choice. But the ones I really feel sorry for are his kids. They don't have any choice."

Not everybody in the family turned away. Our mother and Mitchell visited them in Monsey five or six times a year, sent them money at the beginning of each month to help with the groceries and rent, and took them on annual holiday excursions to Philadelphia, Boston, and Montreal, where they would eat in kosher restaurants and visit parks, museums, and zoos. These forays into the world outside Monsey's borders could sometimes be traumatic. A gang of boys outside a kosher delicatessen in north Philadelphia once pelted the family with crab apples, attempting to knock off my brother's hat, striking my grandmother instead. The police were summoned, but by the time they arrived, the gang had dispersed. A little girl stared at my brother in an aquarium in Montreal and told her parents in a loud voice, "Look—a kike." My brother's children seemed to be absorbing a subliminal message from such encounters. Once our mother took her grandchildren to an insectarium in Philadelphia, where they gathered around the tarantula tank, staring in fear and wonder at the hairy arachnid.

"What's that?" Ruchel asked.

"It's a big spider that likes to hurt people," our mother said.

"Oh," said Ruchel, "a goy."

Tony and his wife began shopping for a home for their burgeoning family in the late 1980s. Mitchell and our mother came up to inspect the place on Blauvelt Road, one of the few houses in Monsey that the family could afford. The old three-bedroomer—previously owned by an observant couple with twelve children—was in terrible shape. Its walls were covered with crayon scribblings, the roof leaked, the pipes had rusted out. Mitchell took charge, filling the role that our father had abdicated. He hired contractors, spent a small fortune on home repairs. Later, at a North Carolina car dealer's, he found them a new Hyundai at a reasonable price and drove the vehicle up to Monsey. He helped my brother arrange an interest-free loan to pay for it from the Gmach Keren Ha Chesed—the Jewish community credit union—and lectured him on auto maintenance. But my brother ignored the advice, and the car began to disintegrate rapidly after that first, bitter New York winter.

My brother's children began to call Mitchell *Opi*—grandpa—and called my mother *Omi*, or grandma. Our father, whose visits were becoming fewer and fewer, was "Uncle Dick." Tony had never explained to his children that our parents had gotten divorced and found new partners, and the children had come to believe that "Dick" was Tony's older brother. Tony apparently never corrected them.

My brother would make periodic interventions into our lives, descending upon us like an angel out of the firmament to comment on our ungodly ways. When our grandmother Mildred died in the fall of 1992, just before Rosh Hashanah, my brother telephoned the funeral home in Hartford. She must not be buried in the dress our father had selected, he told the director, but wrapped in a shroud and placed in a plain pine box—without being embalmed. Otherwise the ceremony would be a violation of Jewish law and he would not attend. "I'm sorry, but I can't do that," the director replied. So Tony called our father. "You live without any Jewish feeling," he said. "Can't you at least let her be buried like a Jew?" But our father wouldn't hear of it. My brother skipped the funeral.

When our grandfather Sam, our mother's father, died some time after Mildred, my brother again attempted to intervene. Sam had willed his body to the University of North Carolina medical school. Tony called our mother in alarm. Didn't she know that the nashama hovers over the body until it decays? Didn't she realize that a body still feels pain as long as the soul is near it? How could she allow her own father to be cut open by scalpels? He urged her to rescind her father's instructions and give him a proper Jewish burial. "As long as his body remains in formaldehyde, his soul can never go up to *himmel*—never."

Just once my brother's intervention did not contain an inherent criticism of our lives. The landlord of our father's building, an ultra-Orthodox Jew, had sent him another eviction notice. Tony visited the man and pleaded with him to relent. The landlord was astonished. "Hammer has a *frum* son?" he exclaimed. My father was given a reprieve.

In 1993, after an intense lobbying effort, I was appointed *Newsweek*'s Nairobi correspondent. The job meant uprooting myself again, yet I was euphoric about the new assignment. On a dreary gray day in January, a month before I left New York, I finally, grudgingly, joined our mother and Mitchell on a brief visit to Monsey, the first time I had visited my brother and his family there since the wedding eight years earlier. I played catch on the lawn with my brother's two small sons, then six and four years old, and had an awkward conversation with Tony in the kitchen about my impending assignment.

"Are you sure you want to go to Africa?" he said, bewildered.

"I'm sure."

"You couldn't go to Europe instead?"

"Why Europe?"

"At least there are Yiddin there."

In Africa, caught up in the dramas of a turbulent continent, I put my brother out of my mind. I seldom talked about him, rarely thought of him. Then, one spring, our mother came to visit me in Nairobi. It was the height of the East African rainy season, the worst time for a safari in the bush. Deep in the Masai Mara game reserve, as we rumbled in my four-wheel-drive Mitsubishi truck over muddy tracks through a lush, undulating savannah of knee-high elephant grass and thorny acacia trees, our mother told me, in fretful tones, that Tony's zealotry was deepening. He had fallen under the spell of a fanatically devout Hasidic rabbi in Brooklyn, she said, a charismatic sect leader who had gone to prison for kidnapping and indoctrinating a teenage boy.

"Your brother's gone over the edge," Mitchell said as the setting sun turned the African sky pink, purple, and gold.

"That's always been his pattern, hasn't it?" I replied.

"I think it may be his endocrine gland," said Mitchell. He was an engineer and a scientist, and it was in his nature to seek out chemical explanations for the mysteries of human behavior.

As I began to fill in the gaps about my brother's life, I found myself talking openly for the first time about his strange odyssey. One of the first questions that people would ask me was whether our family had been religious. The answer I would give was: not in the slightest. Tony's awakening had been a complete aberration. But in a way, it brought our family full circle to the shtetl life of our ancestors in eastern and central Europe six generations ago. In the traditions and religious reverence of his forebears, my brother seemed to find a sense of stability and security that had been painfully absent from both our lives growing up.

The last member of our family to believe that the Torah was, literally, the word of God was our mother's great-grandfather. David Sinberg was born the son of a rabbi near Kiev in 1852. He became a Talmudic scholar, then, at age forty, took a boat from Odessa to New York with his wife and seven children. A Jewish welfare agency sent the family to Fall River, Massachusetts, where he taught Hebrew at a synagogue and wrote letters in Yiddish for illiterate immigrants. Sinberg never learned to speak English and died penniless, in 1930, at the home of his youngest daughter in Providence, Rhode Island. A photograph our mother sent me, taken in the 1920s, shows a stern white-bearded patriarch glowering at the camera. The black overcoat and hat, even the cut of the beard, could have served as models for my brother's.

After Sinberg, the family took the route of so many Jewish immigrants to America: they assimilated rapidly into secular society. Sinberg's daughter Sadie, my great-grandmother, married an itinerant burlesque actor named Al Goldberg, who walked out on the family in 1913, changed his name to A. S. Gilbert, and opened one of the country's first film studios, the Hollywood Film Corporation in Philadelphia. In 1922, Gilbert produced a melodrama called *The Bootlegger*, starring Norma Shearer, then he disappeared, reportedly dying destitute in Los Angeles two decades later.

Our father's family also strayed far from its Jewish roots. Jacob Chaimson, our father's grandfather, a hotel keeper's son, came from the largely Jewish town of Vinnitsa in the Ukraine. Drafted into the czar's army, he escaped to Odessa with his wife, Lena, and eventually made his way to Hartford, Connecticut, where he worked as a fruit peddler and joined the socialist Workmen's Circle. Once a year at High Holy Days, Jake and Lena attended services at an Orthodox synagogue in Hartford. After a few minutes of davening, Jake would join his immigrant friends from the Circle on the sidewalk, smoke Lucky Strikes, thumb through the Yiddish-language *Daily Forward*, and gossip about politics while waiting for his wife to emerge from shul.

Our father was bar mitzvahed at a Reform temple in West Hartford, but he never set foot in a synagogue again after he left home for college in 1946. "As long as there's anti-Semitism in the world, I'll identify myself as Jewish," he said, "but I'm not going to force anything on my children."

It was our mother who felt obligated to send us to Hebrew school, but after that, she said, she would let us decide for ourselves how much Judaism we wanted in our lives. My brother and I both attended Shaaray Tefila, a Reform Jewish temple on East Seventy-second Street and First Avenue, whose head rabbi, a ponytailed young activist named Philip Schechter, angered many congregants by speaking out, early and often, against the war in Vietnam. We learned to read Hebrew, spun dreidels on Chanukkah, went to Passover seders every year at our paternal grandparents' home in West Hartford. When the Israelis, led by one-eyed General Moshe Dayan, defeated the Arabs in the Six-Day War, we ran cheering through the schoolyard with my other Jewish friends at P.S. 6. For several years I chanted the Shemah in Hebrew before I went to sleep each night—"Hear O Israel, the Lord Our God, the Lord is One"—keeping my voice low so that my brother, sleeping a few feet away from me, would not hear me and mock my superstitions.

We lived in the cozy, almost exclusively Jewish world on the Upper East Side of Manhattan. Our single brush with anti-Semitism came in the late 1960s, when our parents inexplicably sent us to a gentile summer camp on the north shore of Long Island, where we were treated as outcasts. There was the bunk mate who kept up a stream of Jewish jokes in my presence, the counselor who called me "Jewboy" and punched me hard, in the gut when I presented him with a nurse's note excusing me from that morning's swimming class because of a stomach ailment. On Sunday night we trudged to the mess hall for a two-hour marathon of Christian hymns and prayers—an experience I learned to dread.

Our father who art in heaven . . . who art . . . who art . . .

"Hey. Hammer doesn't know the Lord's Prayer."

"Our father, the king of the universe . . ."

"How can he not know the Lord's Prayer?"

" 'Cause he's a Jew."

"He should have gone to a Jew camp."

By the time I began to prepare for my bar mitzvah, in the spring of 1970, my interest in Judaism was slipping away. I found myself growing bored by the services, and felt little connection to God. I stopped saying the Shemah and at my bar mitzvah, instead of speaking of my love for the Torah, gave an impassioned speech about Richard Nixon and the Vietnam War. My bar mitzvah luncheon was held at the faded old Gramercy Park Hotel in Manhattan, with entertainment provided by a one-man band. The musician, who must have been seventy, played current pop hits—"Spinning Wheel," "Does Anybody Really Know What Time It Is?"—on his electric organ, as my friends snickered and I sulked. The affair ended when a friend's father drank too much and hurled a wineglass at a floor-to-ceiling mirror in the banquet hall, shattering it into a thousand tiny shards.

Four years later, my brother's bar mitzvah was held in an Orthodox temple in the Riverdale section of the Bronx. It wasn't his idea. Our mother was facing financial hardship at the time, and the rabbis there had offered her the lowest price of all the synagogues in town. But they almost refused to conduct the ceremony when they found out she planned to hold the reception at a non-kosher restaurant in Yonkers—and that shellfish would be served as the main course. Tony handled the all-Hebrew service with aplomb, and the rabbis predicted that he would go far in his Jewish studies. But like me, he had no intention of ever setting foot in synagogue again. For years afterward, whenever the subject came up, Tony bragged that he had "put one over" on the rabbis.

If religion didn't figure highly in our childhoods, family fragmentation did. Looking back, it seems more obvious how differently my brother and I reacted to the instability, the upheaval that started with our parents' divorce. Aged thirteen, nearly four years older than Tony, I was initally devastated, but soon learned to suppress my anger and grief beneath a thickening outer hide. My brother seemed to become more openly lost and vulnerable as time went on.

In conversations about our upbringing, my father admitted to me that they both had known, early on, that the marriage was not going to last. He was on the rebound from a long-term love affair, he told me, when they met on a beach in Nantucket during the summer of 1955. He was twenty-seven years old, had recently abandoned his Columbia University dissertation to take a staff writer job at *Barron's*. My mother was twenty-three, an art history graduate from Mount Vernon, New York, whose parents, lower-middle-class Jews, had divorced during World War II.

By the time of Tony's birth in 1961, the word *divorce* was apparently already in the air. Even today I have little memory of any interaction between our parents. They apparently had little in common, besides a shared love for classical music. According to our father, they were constantly quarreling. I remember only one fight. In the fall of 1965, he bought a Studebaker Avanti—a sleek black "fastback" with a V-8 engine and a speedometer that went up to 200 miles per hour—that created a buzz on our block in Mount Vernon. He took Tony and me for spins around the neighborhood, screeching around corners and waving to admiring teenagers. After a few months our mother made him sell it. Too sporty and too dangerous, she said. He replaced it with a 1966 Chrysler four-door sedan, a clunky green boat, and seethed for weeks.

Our father was often a remote figure to me, but there seemed even less connection between him and Tony. From an early age I dreamed of emulating him. As a reporter for *Fortune*, then *The New York Times*, he was always venturing off on exotic assignments—inside American prisons, to Mississippi to report on the

Voting Rights Act—or locked in his study, chain-smoking Parliaments as he pecked at his Smith Corona electric typewriter. He had the biggest book collection of anyone I knew: thousands of hardcovers, from *The Iliad* to John Gunther to Saul Bellow, that covered nearly every wall in our house. His heroes were liberal politicians and journalists—Robert F. Kennedy, Edward R. Murrow. He was a left-wing Democrat and vocal about it: after Mount Vernon's school board blocked the integration of the city's public school system, he angrily switched us to an experimental Montessori school in Yonkers. We were raised on the protest songs of Woody Guthrie and Pete Seeger, and later, the Beatles, Arlo Guthrie, Led Zeppelin, and Crosby, Stills and Nash. He was planning to work as a speechwriter for Bobby Kennedy during the 1968 presidential campaign—and I remember his stunned expression when I woke him up on a June morning in 1968 and told him I'd heard on the radio that Kennedy had been shot.

Growing up, we were closer to my mother. She had a delicate beauty—soft features, hazel eyes, and a shock of short brown hair. She took us on excursions to the Museum of Modern Art for painting classes, to the Metropolitan Museum to gaze in wonder at the Egyptian mummies and the armor of medieval knights. She bought pastels, watercolors, and construction paper in the vain hope of bringing out some latent artistic talent in us, sitting by my side as I drew portraits of every American president from Washington to John Fitzgerald Kennedy. There was a fragile, vulnerable quality to her as well. Just before we moved to Manhattan in the fall of 1966, her closest friend died after a long struggle with cancer. My mother became deeply depressed. She always seemed to be searching for ways to fulfill herself—art history courses at Columbia University, part-time work in an art gallery, then a full-time job as a technician at the Metropolitan Hospital in Harlem. As my parents' marriage deteriorated, she and my father entered group therapy. There, I discovered years later, she announced to the group that she couldn't tolerate the sound of his voice any longer, and planned to divorce him as soon as the children were grown.

As children, my brother and I had little idea of what was going on. We moved to Manhattan in the fall of 1966. I remember the period as an idyll before the chaos and fragmentation that would define the next decade. We were Upper East Side street kids, on the loose in the city, moving through a succession of escapades—most taking place in the vicinity of Public School 6, the red-brick complex on Eighty-second Street and Madison Avenue, where my brother and I went to school for three years. Early mornings and late afternoons there were stickball and ring-a-levio games in the schoolyard. We bought cherry bombs and M-80s—a pinkie-sized barrel with a powerful charge—from a fireworks dealer and planted them in crannies in the schoolyard, running like hell as the devices exploded with a satisfying boom.

We were companions, but early on my brother seemed to have absorbed the message that he would always be the runner-up in the sibling rivalry between us. I was the creative one, the one with academic promise, the one who captured most of our parents' and grandparents' attention. Tony was the cute, chubby one, the follower, whose gifts—if he had gifts—were obscured beneath his cuddly exterior.

In the winter of 1970 my father spotted a small news item about mass killings of Vietnamese civilians by American troops in a village called My Lai, and landed a $7,000 advance from Little, Brown to write a book about it. He telephoned my brother and me from Alaska on the trip over; sent us postcards from Hong Kong and Saigon. In Quang Nai province, he later recalled, he choppered into a fire base and watched a battle rage between grunts and Vietcong trapped in a bunker; the American troops burned them alive with flame throwers. Watching the slaughter, he told me years later, he realized that he would rather be in the thick of battle than return to a loveless marriage. Days after New Year, 1970, he returned to Saigon, took off his wedding ring, and hurled it into a fountain.

But back in New York my brother and I were still oblivious to the imminent disintegration of our lives. Our father came back from Southeast Asia bearing souvenirs for us—a copy of the *Saigon Post*, a cartridge case, a military map of Vietnam—then vanished into his study to write his book for the next three months. In June, days after my bar mitzvah, we moved to a new apartment in Riverdale, a largely Jewish suburban enclave in the northwest Bronx. It was a luxury high-rise perched on the banks of the Hudson River, with doormen in smart uniforms, crystal chandeliers in the lobby, a swimming pool, and tennis courts. After four years of sharing a cramped bedroom on East Eightieth Street, Tony and I now each had our own huge room facing the Hudson. For a week it was heaven.

Then, on a Saturday morning, our father walked into my bedroom in our new apartment and shut the door. My brother and I were sitting on the floor, playing a board game called Stratomatic Baseball. The sun was streaming through the windows.

He sat on my bed, folded his hands together, and rested them on his knees. "Do you remember last week," he said, "when you told me you wished I would move out of the house?" I felt a wave of panic. It had been a remark made in the heat of anger, following some now forgotten argument.

"I didn't mean it," I said, staring up at him from the floor.

"I'm leaving your mother," he said.

The words didn't sink in at first. "What do you mean?"

"I'm going to spend the night at Aunt Patti's, and then I'm

going to move into an apartment in Manhattan. I'll see you every other weekend. And if you ever need to talk to me, all you have to do is pick up the telephone."

"But we just moved in," I protested. "How can you be leaving?"

"Your mother and I don't get along," he said. "Have you noticed that we never hug or kiss? Would you rather have us stay together and be unhappy?"

"Yes," I said, beginning to cry.

"It can't be like that. This is going to be better for everybody. You'll see."

My brother and I sat speechlessly in my room for the next half hour, listening to our father opening drawers and closets, packing a small suitcase for his journey. Then he was gone. The next weekend he returned to pick up some of his belongings. Our mother rushed to the door, called him "darling" and kissed him full on the lips—the first time, I realized, I had seen her display any affection toward him in years.

"Can I get my boxes, Nina?" he said.

Her demeanor changed in an instant. Suddenly, she began hurling obscenities at him—words I had never heard our mother use before. Yanking open the closet, she flung shoes, shoe trees, photo albums, coats, ripping the closet apart. My brother and I stood observing the scene in terror.

"The kids are watching," he said.

"Get out of my house!" she screamed. I ran into my room and pressed my face into my pillow. In the next room, all that morning I could hear our mother weeping.

And suddenly, everything was different. Our father settled into a bachelor apartment on West Twenty-third Street, and almost simultaneously his book, *One Morning in the War: The Tragedy at Son My* arrived in the bookstores. Overnight, we were the sons of a celebrity. *The New York Times* and *The New Yorker* praised the book. *Life* magazine included it on its list of the three most important works of nonfiction of 1970. There were book signings, lectures, an appearance on *The Dick Cavett Show*. A few weeks later, our father took my brother and me on a walk through Central Park and told us he was going to be married again.

"Her name is Arlene," he said.

I had seen the photograph of a beautiful auburn-haired young woman on the night table of his bachelor apartment. But I had been too embarrassed, too worried, to ask him about her. "How can you be getting married again?" I asked. "You're not even divorced."

He had met her at a literary party at the Coffee House in Manhattan, hosted by a Soviet-American friendship organization, only days before he had left my mother. He was a guest speaker; she was a rising theatrical star and Russian translator. Twenty-six years old, she was warm, gregarious, full of life. I liked her from the moment I met her, but I had been holding out an irrational hope that our father would return to live with us in Riverdale—and I saw Arlene as a threat to my dreams of a re-united home.

Arlene's mother was a churchgoing Methodist, but they had opted for a Jewish wedding. They went to see Rabbi Schechter, the anti-war rabbi who had bar mitzvahed me. What are your beliefs? Schechter asked our father. "I don't have any beliefs," he replied. The rabbi told Arlene he was counting on her to bring to their children a recognition of the importance of the Jewish faith. On a Monday evening the immediate family gathered in Schechter's book-lined library at Temple Shaaray Tefila. My brother and I signed the *ketubah*, the marriage contract. Then they drove off to Gurney's Inn on Montauk, Long Island, for their honeymoon, leaving me feeling confused and betrayed.

While my brother seemed to retreat inward, I cursed and cried and let the world know that I would not accept this shattering of our family. Four months after our father left, our mother moved us into a smaller place in a stark red-brick high-rise overlooking the Henry Hudson Parkway. Gone were the river views, the swimming pool. My brother and I went back to sharing a single room. I took one look at the narrow little chamber—with a three-foot gap between our beds—and fled the apartment in dismay. I was angry at the world, at our father for turning his back on us, at our mother for taking us down several notches, and at my brother for his equanimity.

"How come you never say anything?" I asked him one evening as we sat watching *The Partridge Family*. "Don't you hate Dad for what he did?"

Tony, who was nine years old, shrugged, which only made me angrier.

Our mother did her best to keep the family together. To make me happy, she walled off the dining alcove beside the kitchen and turned it into a tiny third bedroom. I would wake up at seven o'clock every morning to hear her brewing coffee before she took the bus to her grueling job hooking indigent patients up to heart monitors at the Metropolitan Hospital, a bleak public facility at the edge of Harlem. Then I would walk to class at Horace Mann, the boys' private school I attended in Riverdale, trying to pretend that nothing had happened. She returned home around seven o'clock at night—after an hour ride at rush hour on the Riverdale Express Bus—weary, dispirited, and cooked us dinner. Soon she began dating again, and the home-cooked meals were often replaced by Swanson TV dinners: rubbery Salisbury steaks, dollops of mashed potatoes, and tasteless peach cobblers neatly placed in segmented aluminum trays.

Tony and I learned to adapt to the stark new reality of our

lives. We played "knee football"—moving the furniture aside in the living room and scrambling around on our knees while carrying a miniature pigskin, ignoring our downstairs neighbor's furious pounding on the ceiling. We played thousands of games of Stratomatic baseball and football: fiendishly complex board games with statistically calibrated player cards representing the entire rosters of NFL and Major League Baseball teams. We would roll the dice for hours, entering the statistics into spiral notebooks, playing fifty-game baseball seasons with all twenty-four Major League teams.

In the early 1970s marijuana made its first appearance at Horace Mann School, and a group would assemble every morning at a small park across from the campus called David's Corner. When I was fifteen a friend produced a joint as we played pool in the rear of Lou and Tito's Luncheonette beneath the elevated train tracks of the Broadway line. We smoked it in Van Cortland Park in the northwest Bronx that afternoon, and when I came home in the early evening, I nearly nodded off at the dinner table. My eleven-year-old brother studied me, sensing something odd about my behavior. Soon I was smoking marijuana before and after—even during—school. The drug gave me an identity, and made me feel superior to my brother. It was at that time that we began to drift apart.

A year after the divorce, the *New York Times Week in Review* section sent my father to Fort Benning, Georgia, to cover the court martial of Lieutenant William Calley, the American army officer accused of organizing the slaughter at My Lai. He spent four and a half months filing weekly dispatches to the *Times*, and turned his reporting into a third book, *The Court-Martial of Lieutenant Calley*. He was now one of the country's most prominent critics of the war in Vietnam. He won the *New York Times* Publishing Award and was nominated for a National Book Award. A movie he produced and wrote, *Interviews with*

My Lai Veterans, won the 1971 Academy Award for best short documentary. He was my hero and my role model, even though I hated him for what he had done to us. I marched in anti-war rallies, lectured my classmates on the evil of our involvement in Southeast Asia. Every other weekend my brother and I rode the Riverdale Express bus down to our father's one-bedroom apartment on West Eighty-sixth Street and Columbus Avenue. Arlene took us to Broadway musicals, brought us to the dressing rooms to meet her friends in the casts of *Fiddler on the Roof* and *Grease*. On spring and fall weekends her father, a champion yachtsman, took us sailing beneath the Verrazano Bridge and into the Atlantic Ocean on his twenty-eight-foot sloop. Then we returned to our tiny apartment in the Bronx.

I wanted to escape Riverdale. The men who would come to our apartment to take my mother on dates only accentuated the sense of fragmentation. One night a husky gray-haired stranger knocked at the door. He sat on the couch in the living room and called my brother and me over while our mother got ready in her bedroom.

"You like baseball, young fellow?" he said.

"I love baseball," I said.

"You like Hank Aaron?"

"Yes."

"Willie Mays?"

"Who doesn't like Willie Mays?"

"Great ballplayers, aren't they?"

"Yes."

"All the best ball players are niggers," he said.

"Huh?"

"Niggers. Have you ever wondered why that was?"

Life at home often became unbearable. Small disagreements between my mother and me would escalate into exchanges of foul language and, sometimes, violence. Tony would watch these battles silently, hovering on the sidelines, uncertain when—or how—to intervene. After one of the most violent of these episodes, my brother rushed to the telephone and called our father, begging for help. Things became so volatile that our mother even took us to see a family therapist. The session ended cathartically, with our mother and I sobbing, hugging, and promising to make a better effort to get along. My brother sat impassively and watched.

THE HAMLET WHERE MY BROTHER DECIDED TO spend his life is nestled just south of the Catskill Mountains, a few miles west of the Hudson River, in a verdant region of rolling hills and forests. Named after the local Munsee Indians, the town a century ago was a sleepy rural village of apple orchards, Protestant churches, and Victorian and Edwardian mansions built by wealthy merchants and farmers. But the main spur of the Erie Railroad line linking Jersey City with Chicago ran right through Monsey, and by World War I the wooded hamlet was becoming a popular vacation retreat for religious Jews from the New York metropolitan area. The ultra-Orthodox stayed in modest bungalow colonies with communal kitchens, known as *kucheleins*, or in country inns tucked away in the woods. At the end of the summer they went home, and Monsey went back to being a gentile town.

Then in 1942 an ultra-Orthodox rabbi from Brooklyn named Rabbi Shraga Feival Mendlowitz bought a crumbling brick Victorian mansion with matching medieval-style turrets at the corner of Maple Avenue and

Main Street. Mendlowitz converted the building—a defunct military academy—into Monsey's first yeshiva. The yeshiva, called Beis Medrish Elyon, became a magnet for Talmudic scholars across America. Soon Monsey was reborn.

In the 1950s the building of the Palisades Parkway and the Tappan Zee Bridge across the Hudson River suddenly made Monsey easily accessible from New York City. Thousands of ultra-Orthodox Jewish migrants fled their neighborhoods in Brooklyn, as the encroachment of the Brooklyn-Queens Expressway and construction of low-income housing projects on the edges of Williamsburg, Borough Park, and Crown Heights made urban life increasingly untenable for them. The new suburbanites bought up old summer bungalows and turned them—often illegally—into multi-family houses. They also converted fading old hotels like the Monsey Palace into yeshivas and synagogues, and started community services such as Hatzolah, the volunteer ambulance corps.

Monsey's first Orthodox wave was largely made up of Talmudic scholars from the Litvisher sect, but the population quickly diversified. First came Rabbi Jacob Joseph Twersky, a Hasidic spiritual leader from Skvira in the Ukraine, by way of Williamsburg, Brooklyn. Twersky bought a 130-acre dairy farm just north of Monsey in 1956 and moved there with sixty families. The Skvira Hasidim called their village New Square, declared independence from the town of Ramapo after a bitter legal battle, and passed a raft of religiously inspired zoning laws and ordinances—including banning traffic from all streets on the Sabbath. That legal victory really put the area on the map. Next came the Pupahs, the Bobovs, and the Satmar Hasidim. And in the early 1980s the Viznitz Hasidic sect from the Carpathian Mountains of Rumania made Monsey its new world headquarters. Today, Monsey is like an ultra-Orthodox prism, refracting what seems to the outside world to be a solid band of black into its various components: 30 percent Hasidim, 40 percent Litvishers, with a smattering of Sephardim, Vin Jews, and modern Orthodox Jews as well.

On a Saturday afternoon in December, my brother led me on a walking tour of Monsey. We strolled along Blauvelt Road, what locals call the *platz*—the older, poorer end of town. Most houses here had been built before World War II, and a few of the original residents were still living in them. They included my brother's next-door neighbor, an octogenarian Lutheran widow who served as the family's Shabbos goy—the gentile who handled emergencies that arose during the Sabbath. Besides her, the only other non-Jews in the neighborhood were five families of recent Slavic immigrants who lived in a new Cape Cod-style apartment block across the street. They kept to themselves. On warm days they would sit on the back lawn, playing eastern European music, barbecuing, and speaking in harsh, unfamiliar tongues. Everyone else on Blauvelt Road was ultra-Orthodox, and as we wandered down the street, my brother kept up a running patter about his neighbors: "Those are the Rosenmans. He's a bus driver," he said, pointing at one dilapidated bungalow covered with aluminum siding and set on a weedy lawn. "They have fourteen children. The Goldbaums live there—twelve children. Over there are the Mandelbaums—nineteen children, baruch Hashem."

Just west of Blauvelt Road, the neighborhood became more affluent. We passed tidy ranch houses, with sports utility vehicles in the driveways and well-manicured lawns, and the occasional home-delivered copy of *The New York Times* lying beside the front door. To the north lay Manny Weldler Park, a public recreation center with tennis courts and baseball fields and playgrounds, and on a rise above it, a new development called Concord, where the wealthiest Orthodox families in Monsey lived. Here were sprawling homes with domed atriums, indoor swimming pools, and manicured gardens that swept upward toward still pristine woods. My brother seemed to take pleasure in strolling through Concord's immaculate streets. "Whenever we see that a Yid has made good, it makes us happy," he said. Farther north, Monsey petered out into cow pastures, corn fields, and in the distance, gently rising hills.

Perched high in telephone poles on certain streets, I noticed, were miniature doorway-like structures: each consisted of two wooden side posts and a cross post resting atop them. The little doorways, my brother explained, formed the *eirev*, a perimeter that ran around much of the village. It is considered a mitzvah on Shabbos not to carry objects from a private domain, such as a house, into a public domain, such as a street, but the eirev turned all of the area that it enclosed into one vast private domain allowing the orthodox to elude the prohibition. The original eirev was laid out around much of the town by a modern Orthodox rabbi in Monsey in the 1970s. But it was a subject of bitter argument. Many ultra-Orthodox residents of Monsey claimed that the miniature doorways did not correspond to precise Talmudic requirements, and they refused to recognize them. There were at least two other competing eirevs in Monsey carved out by ultra-Orthodox rabbis. The battle of the eirevs was one of many obscure disputes, I discovered, that simmered beneath Monsey's placid surface.

"I'll tell you a little secret," my brother said. We had been walking through the hamlet for nearly an hour, and I had asked him to tell me about what had happened seventeen years earlier, after I had left him in Jerusalem. "Right after I got to Israel, I put a note in the Wailing Wall. I said, 'God, if you exist, show me a sign.'"

The admission surprised me, since I remembered how contemptuous my brother had been of organized religion, and how deeply skeptical he had seemed about the existence of God. "When did you see the sign?"

"When I walked in the doors of Ohr Somayach."

He had been penniless, adrift, and increasingly unhappy about his job in Fefferberg's Restaurant in Jerusalem, he told me. So that summer he drifted down to the Red Sea for a week and camped on the beach with an American backpacker. He later encountered the backpacker outside Ohr Somayach, where the young man had signed up for classes. Not wanting to leave Israel just yet, and figuring that the yeshiva might provide him with a chance to live for free, my brother signed up too. He cut a deal with Baruch Levine, committing himself to a three-week stay in the dormitory—if the yeshiva would help him pay for his plane ticket back to America.

My brother entered the yeshiva expecting to encounter a den full of cultists. Instead, he told me, he felt unexpectedly at home. Until Tony arrived at Ohr Somayach, he had imagined that nearly all ultra-Orthodox Jews resembled the Hasidim he had gaped at on West Forty-seventh Street in Manhattan and in Me'a Sha'arim, the old Orthodox ghetto. But the message at the yeshiva, Tony said, was: "You don't have to wear the long peyyes. You can be a lawyer, a professor, a politico, a computer analyst. It doesn't interfere with the fact that your life is as a Jew."

What he heard in his classes enthralled him. The message that had seemed so remote and irrelevant to me struck my brother with the clarity of an epiphany. As his philosophy teacher elucidated the familiar story of the Jews—God had revealed to the wandering Israelites the Torah on Mount Sinai and entered with them into a sacred covenant—my brother could feel a dawning awareness of his destiny, he told me. He was no insignificant speck in an indifferent universe, but a part of a great history. He was an acolyte in a nation of priests.

The choice, his teachers told him, belonged to him. God would not force the Jews to live according to His Word. God did not intend for His people to be chickens or horses, automatons programmed blindly to obey their instincts. He had deliberately endowed mankind with a free will. At the same time, God made clear the consequences of turning away from Him. God held Mount Sinai over the heads of the Israelites, and He told them, "If you take the Torah, good. If you don't take it, this will be your burial place."

Then my brother began to read the Gemorah, the ancient rabbinical commentaries that, along with the Mishnah, make up the Talmud. If one ox gores another man's ox, who pays? How much should the damages be? One tsaddik had likened the study of Gemorah to "tickling" the nashama. After a month at Ohr Somayach, my brother recalled, he wore a yarmulke on the street for the first time. "I went out to lunch with Ronnie and a friend from the army, and they made fun of me. Ronnie said, 'What are you wearing that for?' But I didn't take it off."

As I listened to my brother describe his religious awakening at Ohr Somayach, I knew that I would never fully comprehend it. I could sense his excitement, I could summarize the arguments that swayed him, yet I could never experience the epiphany he felt. I sensed that for him, the lure of ultra-Orthodox Judaism was as much emotional as it was intellectual. I sensed that his acceptance of God had also come out of deep wellsprings of pain.

Three months into his stay at Ohr Somayach, my brother's new resolve began to falter. Although he believed that the Torah was the truth, he told me, he could not shut out the siren call of the secular world. He returned home to America. But when he arrived at Hobart, he wandered the campus feeling lost and alienated. He discovered that all the belongings that he had put in a campus storage room before going to Israel—a bicycle, electric typewriter, piles of books and papers—had disappeared. He interpreted the theft as a sign from God. After three days he boarded the bus back to New York City without bothering to tell his friends and professors good-bye.

In the early winter chill, my brother and I climbed a footpath leading to the campus of Ohr Somayach, the most prestigious yeshiva in Monsey, located a mile north of his home. I had asked him to show me where he had lived during his first months in the hamlet, after his flight from Hobart and the secular world. We strolled across snow-dusted lawns, passed two newly constructed dormitories built for a rapidly expanding population of baal tshuvas, and arrived in front of a sprawling red-brick synagogue complex. Despite the cold, dozens of yeshiva students were gathered at the entrances of the dorms and the shul. I listened to their conversations and could immediately tell they were engaged in Talmudic debate. Memories of my brief stay at Ohr Somayach in Jerusalem came flooding back. Here were the same earnest young visages, the same scruffy beards, ponytails, jeans, and tsitsis, the same internal struggles externalized as sartorial confusion.

Ohr Somayach was little more than a campsite during that winter of 1982 when my brother arrived by bus from New York: eight rough cottages scattered about a clearing in the woods, part of a former summer bungalow colony built before World War II. There were two dozen American and British baal tshuvas enrolled at the yeshiva, my brother remembered, including a seventy-five-year-old man named Lublin who had come to retrieve his psychologist son from what he had called the "cult" and wound up becoming a member himself.

We stopped before a dilapidated gray-shingle shack next to the highway. It was tiny, nearly windowless, and made me think of photographs of the Unabomber's sanctuary in the wilds of Montana. "This was where I spent the first three months," my brother told me.

It had been grueling at first, he recalled. The rooms were spartan. Meals were communal and unenticing. Three times a day he would trudge up to the tiny synagogue through the snow to daven. He would spend hours burrowed in the library, immersed in the thirty-six volumes of Talmud. He learned the mechanisms of animal sacrifices in the Temple and the laws regarding blessings, repayment of debts, property disputes, marriage contracts, and divorce contracts. How many *zuz* must a groom pay for his betrothed? What contractual language must be employed to emancipate a slave? He memorized the judicial code of the ancient rabbinical court of Israel, known as the Sanhedrin: blasphemers were to be tossed to the ground from a twelve-foot precipice, then stoned to death by the hurling of boulders on the chest and head. Strangulation was the penalty for those who had adulterous sex with the daughter of a koher, a Jewish priest in the holy temple.

But memorizing the minutiae of the Jewish canon was only part of it. My brother had set about remaking his character, trait by trait, according to the moral principles set forth in the Torah. The tsaddikim wrote that a Jew must suppress all feelings of envy toward other men, refrain from calumny, laziness, and worry over material pursuits. A Jew must rid himself of his earthly ambitions, trust the Blessed One to grant his needs and his food, and not pursue things which would deter him from Torah study. When in doubt, he should remember the words of Tehillim, the Psalms of David: "But he who trusts in God will be surrounded by loving kindness." He must conquer his anger, the tsaddikim said, because anger blots out prayer. And, above all, he must do tshuva— repent—for the transgressions he has committed against man and God.

Sometimes he wasn't sure he had the inner strength for it all, he told me. My brother would sit in the dining room of his cottage, reading paperback editions of Brecht's plays and smoking little Indian cigarettes. On Sundays he would hitchhike on the New York State Thruway to visit a rock musician friend at SUNY Purchase, or ride the bus down to Manhattan to visit friends from Performing Arts. He'd spend the weekend at my father's apartment, watching NFL games on television, frequenting his favorite Greenwich Village bars; then he returned to Monsey feeling more conflicted than ever. He would skip davening, suffering through a week of second thoughts before recommitting himself to the rigors of Ohr Somayach.

He told the rabbis he was wavering. "The one who struggles makes himself stronger in the end," they told him. His seventy-five-year-old classmate told him it was time to commit himself—or leave the yeshiva. "The only thing anyone ever got from sitting on a fence post was a butt filled with splinters," he said. One weekend my brother visited Arlene's parents, Norman and Martha Nadel, who lived on Staten Island. Norman, a prominent theater critic, had been close to both of us when we were growing up, and had presided over Tony's 1974 bar mitzvah. He looked askance at Tony's dalliance with religious life, but he was not the type of person to force his values on somebody else. "Listen," he simply told my brother. "You've got to make a decision."

I listened to my brother's story in astonishment. Until we were reunited in Monsey, I had always assumed that his journey into ultra-Orthodoxy had been a relatively painless process. But now I was beginning to understand what a struggle it had been. I picked up a volume of the Talmud, felt light-headed as I scanned the rune-like rabbinical commentaries on commentaries on commentaries—and imagined my brother poring over the ancient texts, battling eye strain and tedium. I pictured him davening in synagogue for endless hours, trying to conjure up the face of God out of nothingness. I no longer regarded Tony's transformation as an escape into bliss. In a way, I thought, it was a reflection of my brother's fortitude, not his weakness.

A few months after my brother's arrival at Ohr Samayach, he told me, Rabbi Raphael Rosenman, a quiet Talmudic scholar with thirteen children, invited him to dinner with his family. The occasion was Purim, the holiday that celebrates Esther's foiling of Haman's genocidal plot against the Jews of Persia. The rabbi's wife, Sheindi, was appalled by my brother's appearance, he recalled: long greasy hair, dirty jeans, sneakers, and a torn T-shirt. How could someone be so slovenly and yet hope to succeed as a Talmud scholar? she asked her husband.

"Trust me," Rosenman told her. "He has a good nashama."

Before long my brother was a regular guest for Shabbos. He began studying the Talmud privately with Rosenman, who lived in constant pain from an inoperable malformed disk in his neck. The rabbi would sit for hours with his chin resting in the strap of a weighted pulley that eased the pressure on his upper vertebrae, barely able to move, yet he would read the texts from nine in the morning until midnight. "I have nothing from this world," Rosenman said. "I'm in pain the whole day long." My brother redoubled his efforts to master the Talmud.

His year-long struggle came to a climax at Yom Kippur in 1982, the Jews' day of atonement. The final prayer, at sundown, is called n'eilah, or the closing of the gates, the last opportunity of the year for a Jew to repent his sins. It was the moment, my brother decided, for him to commit to the religious life or walk away forever. "Yes or no?" he asked himself. He thought about the inner strength of Rabbi Rosenman. He thought about the truth of the Torah and the Talmud. "Yes or no?" he asked himself again. "Yes" came his answer. Then he walked up the pathway to shul and davened more fervently than he ever had done in his life.

In the weeks that followed, my brother cut his hair, threw out his jeans, started growing side curls, and adopted a Hebrew name. Rabbi Rosenman chose it for him. Tony would henceforth be known as Tuvia. It meant "the Blessed One of God."

Days after my Sabbath visit to Monsey, I sat in our father's apartment on East Ninety-second Street, looking through photo albums from his two years in California, trying to jar my memory about that period of our lives: the last idyll for him and Arlene before everything turned sour.

I flipped past photographs of our family trip in the summer of 1973 to John Muir Forest and Big Sur, past photos of the state fair in Grants Pass, Oregon, where my brother and I caught our father stealing a smoke behind a roller coaster, years after he'd sworn to Arlene that he'd given up the habit. I studied photos too of their three-bedroom rented home on stilts perched high in the Hollywood Hills, with panoramic views of the smog-choked city of Los Angeles, and a black Audi in their garage. During the summer of the Watergate hearings, while I taught myself to type and watched John Dean on television and my brother rode horseback on the beach at a Topanga Canyon day camp, our father secreted himself in his study, fashioning an eight-hundred-page manuscript that he believed would cement his place in the front rank of America's journalists-turned-authors.

The book was a biography of the Depression-era Mafia boss Lucky Luciano, one of the most ruthless and powerful criminals in American history. After he was exiled to Italy in the 1950s, Luciano met frequently with a Hollywood producer and former radio comedy writer named Martin Gosch, who wanted to make a movie about his life. The ex-Mafia boss died in Gosch's arms of a heart attack at Naples airport in 1962—and exactly one decade later, after reading our father's award-winning book, *The Court-Martial of Lieutenant Calley*, Gosch asked him to collaborate on a biography of the gangster. Gosch produced notes from hundreds of hours of conversations with Luciano, claiming the gangster had made him swear to keep the material secret until ten years after his death.

Our father was leery of Gosch, a marginal figure in Hollywood, but when a search through his background failed to turn up any evidence of wrongdoing, he decided to proceed with the collaboration. Six publishing houses bid on the book, and Gosch and our father signed a lucrative hardcover contract with Little, Brown, with the promise of hundreds of thousands dollars more through the sale of paperback and movie rights. Our father asked the *Times* for a leave of absence to write the book, but was refused. Faced with a choice of leaving the paper or abandoning his outside project, he quit and moved to California to begin the collaboration.

The summer of 1974 was a time of euphoria, of great expectations: Richard Nixon was gone from the White House, and *The Last Testament of Lucky Luciano* was shaping up to be a near-certain best seller. That fall our father and Arlene moved back to New York City after a two-year absence, and rented the apartment on Ninety-second Street and Lexington Avenue. Soon after their return, Arlene discovered she was pregnant. We all went to Sardi's—the legendary restaurant in the heart of the Broadway theater district—to celebrate their good fortune. Then we waited for our father to hit the jackpot.

Our excitement grew as the publicity blitz began: a full-page ad in *The New York Times* for an excerpt in the October issue of *Penthouse*. "The Godfather Talks," said the big bold letters above a portrait of the gangster. "Luciano put his incredible life story on tape," the ad declared. "He had the tapes locked in a secret bank vault. And now for the first time anywhere, you (and the police) can read the real life story of the real life Godfather in his own words." The Book of the Month Club and the Playboy Book Club both made *The Last Testament of Lucky Luciano* their main selection for January. New American Library secured paperback rights for nearly a million dollars, one of the biggest deals in the history of publishing. There was talk of a big-budget movie.

But the bubble was soon to burst, and the denouement would send our family reeling. There was one problem with the Luciano story: there were no tapes. Luciano had refused to allow Gosch to record his voice, and the producer had been obliged to write everything down in notebooks. *Penthouse* editors were apologetic, our father recalled years later, blaming the mistake on an advertising agency copywriter with a vivid imagination. But now our father was faced with a potentially bigger problem. There were no notebooks either. In late 1973, after a falling out with our father, Gosch died of a heart attack on a plane to New York. After his death, his widow moved out of their house and incinerated her late husband's files, including all of his notes from his thirty meetings with Luciano in Rome and Naples.

One morning in December 1974—on the eve of *The Last Testament*'s publication—my brother and I picked up *The New York Times* at home in Riverdale. There, on the front page below the fold, was a chilling headline: "Questions Are Raised on Lucky Luciano Book." The piece was potentially ruinous. The authors, the story reported, had Luciano participating in meetings at a time when he was locked up in a federal prison. The mobster was quoted describing events that occurred two years after his death. The implication was clear: Gosch had fabricated his "interviews" with Luciano in Italy, then enlisted our father in the scheme.

It was a time of uncertainty, of deepening panic. The dream was threatening to slip away, and during the winter of 1975 our father met repeatedly with his attorneys and editors, desperately trying to salvage his book—and his reputation. My brother and I were kept at arm's length from the growing mess. But we were both aware of the stress that the accusations were causing him.

Little, Brown decided to go ahead with the publication of *The Last Testament of Lucky Luciano*. Our father led the counterattack. He presented notarized documents, notes, and letters from the gangster—verified by handwriting analysts—that proved the two men had a close friendship and a deal to make a book and a movie. But the irrevocable fact remained: the tapes did not exist. The notes had been destroyed. The damage had been done. Soon afterward, the paperback deal collapsed. Some colleagues came to my father's defense, but even their support was qualified. "I leave for others the questions about the book's authenticity, and I believe that, whatever Gosch's deceptions, Hammer was not a party to them," wrote Victor Navasky in the Sunday *Times* Book Review. "But the returns, as politicians and publishers say, are not in."

My brother and I would visit our father and Arlene in Manhattan, and sense that the world was teetering around them. We would listen to him rage against Martin Gosch's widow and his former colleagues at *The New York Times*. He was convinced that one of the paper's editors, a longtime enemy, had deliberately set out to undermine the book out of jealousy and spite. He believed that other Mafia writers had ganged up on him because he had dared to tread on their turf. "I don't have to tell you the damage that all this is doing," he wrote to the editor of the *Book Review*, a longtime colleague. "Maybe to some it seems like news, or like fun. But to someone who finds himself in the middle, it ain't."

Our father never told us how much harm the scandal was causing. He didn't have to. He parted ways with his literary agent. His life became consumed by an endless libel suit filed by the mobster's mistress, and his book advances and royalties were held in escrow as the case dragged through the courts. The sense of excitement, of possibility that had gripped our family in the early 1970s—the days of *One Morning in the War* and *The Court-Martial of Lieutenant Calley*—began to fade. Money worries and an ongoing fight with Gosch's widow over legal bills became the leitmotifs of our lives.

I was sure that my father had been guilty of, at worst, a touch of naivete in his dealings with Gosch, and the pain of watching him being battered by damaging accusations was difficult to bear. I could sense their troubles in the letters I received from the Princeton University comptroller, threatening me with suspension if fees were not paid. I saw the financial squeeze in the apartment's fraying furniture, peeling wallpaper, the thrift-shop clothing in which they dressed my little sister. I saw it in their frantic searches for a misplaced bus transfer or subway token, the rummaging along Third Avenue in search of cast-off chairs and dressers for Allison's bedroom. After a while I found it hard to remember a time when they were not struggling, and their threadbare lives instilled in me a tight-fistedness, a determination never to end up in such a situation. Our father would eventually rebuild his career, winning Edgar Awards and producing a steady turnout of true-crime books and other works of nonfiction. But that recovery would take several long years. In my brother, who lived with them during a time of prolonged hardship, I can imagine that the ordeal only served to exacerbate his feelings of instability, his sense that the world was a frightening, unpredictable place.

The year before the Luciano scandal disrupted all of our lives, my brother decided that he wanted to become an actor. Encouraged by Arlene, he applied to the theater department at the High School of Performing Arts in Manhattan—later to be the setting for the movie *Fame*. For his audition he performed a short monologue from William Inge's *Dark at the Top of the Stairs*, at Arlene's suggestion, playing the part of Sammy Flood, an introverted Jewish teenager who commits suicide later in the play. Arlene worked on the monologue with him for weeks, helping him find the connection between Sammy's vulnerability and aspects of his own character. Only sixty of six hundred applicants were admitted as actors to the school, a springboard for the finest undergraduate theater, music, and dance programs in the country, including Juilliard Academy. My brother—to his surprise and delight—learned in the fall of 1974 that he was one of them.

He was thirteen years old, and it was the first real validation of his abilities that he had ever received. All his life he had been living in my shadow. I was the one who attended the elite private school, albeit on scholarship, the one who basked in the praise of doting grandparents, the one who drilled into him that he was talentless, hopeless, a shadow of who I was. And now he had achieved something of his own. Looking back, I realize that I never even bothered to congratulate him.

The High School of Performing Arts was located in a red-brick five-story building—originally a women's prison—on Sixth Avenue and West Forty-sixth Street. One hundred eighty students, blacks, Jews, Puerto Ricans, Chinese, an astonishingly diverse array of talent, met and mingled in a hothouse environment where self-expression and flamboyance were prized. In my brother's first year there, friends remembered, a willowy teenager named Roy began wearing lipstick to class, then one day—during a theatrical exercise—removed his pants to reveal that he had on a pair of panty hose. By senior year, Roy had become Rose. There were no sports teams, no clubs, nothing to distract students from their dream: a life on the stage.

My brother fell in with a clique of fellow actors—the Method Acting Team, they called themselves—a circle of prima donnas who lived and breathed the theater. They went to plays and movies nearly every night, then huddled in coffee shops, trading jokes, bits of dialogue and critiques of the actors' performances. "Brando is the finest actor ever, finer than Olivier," Tony would say, or "Eartha Kitt is a more feline Catwoman than Julie Newmar." Tony could talk authoritatively about how Anton Chekhov pioneered the short-story form, or give a discourse on the career of the actress Rosemary Harris. Plays and playwrights and actors were virtually their only frame of reference. Many years later, one of his best friends remembered how he would bring my brother to hysterics by parodying Richard Burton in Peter Schaffer's Broadway hit *Equus*: "With one particular horse, named Nugget, he embraces," he would intone in a mock Welsh accent, and Tony would roar with laughter.

They would smoke pot at a fountain across from the school, and dance down Forty-sixth Street fencing with foils lifted from the props department. One day my brother and his friends staged a mugging, while other students dressed in police uniforms took statements from passersby on Broadway. They disrobed mannikins at Bloomingdale's, hurled brownies from the school rooftop at moviegoers waiting in line at the cinema across the street.

It was all good fun, and Tony was always in the center of it. Yet many years later, his friends remembered that Tony had about him a sense of unhappiness, of frustration and insecurity. They remembered him as "the clown," "the foil," as "goofy," as "buzzing with nervous energy." They remembered him as an enthusiast who encouraged his friends and made them feel good about themselves—but who received little encouragement from them in return. In acting classes he, like everyone else, craved the parts of Shakespearean heroes and Brando-like rebels, but he was often shunted into the roles that nobody else wanted: sweet-natured, vulnerable Jews. He played a similar part within his clique. He seemed anxious and unsure of himself. One friend remembers him lying in the sun on Montauk on a freezing day in early spring, shirt off, teeth chattering, trying desperately to get a tan. Many sensed that Tony was in a great deal of pain—about our parents' divorce, about his bad complexion. But nobody, they recalled, ever took him aside to bolster his self-confidence.

In the spring of 1976, at the end of my freshman year at Princeton University, and midway through Tony's second year at the High School of Performing Arts, our mother abruptly announced that she was moving to Paris with her best friend, June. By that point there wasn't much keeping her in New York City: a dreary, draining job at the public hospital, a string of unsatisfying relationships. Now that I was in college and Tony was spending many nights with our father and stepmother in Manhattan, she felt free to make a clean break.

I was far away from the family's troubles at that point, but looking back on it now, I can imagine my brother's state of mind. He must have felt cast adrift, uncertain of where he belonged in the world, as he shuttled between a mother who felt rootless at the time and a father who was fighting financial crisis after crisis.

In early summer, my brother arrived unannounced at the door of our aunt Patti's Riverdale apartment, where she lived with her second husband, a housing court judge, and her two teenage daughters. Patti remembers that he looked forlorn, alone.

"Can I stay for dinner?" he asked.

"Where's your mother?"

"She's gone to France," Tony said. Our mother had sold or put in storage most of what she owned and boarded a plane to Paris with a few items of clothing. Although my father and stepmother had offered to take him in, he was sleeping in an empty apartment, he told Patty. On the floor.

That summer Patti was serving as the Bronx borough coordinator of Congresswoman Bella Abzug's mayoral primary race against Edward Koch, Mario Cuomo, and several other Democrats. The next morning she took Tony with her to Abzug's campaign headquarters—a trailer on gritty Kingsbridge Avenue in the East Bronx—and signed him up as a volunteer. He was nervous, shy, and unsure of himself, Patti remembers, the kind of kid who seemed to bring out everyone's parental instincts. She put him to work distributing campaign leaflets at subway stations. But within a few weeks she noticed a certain flair for politics. Soon he was working on Abzug's "advance team"—escorting the candidate to the far reaches of the borough. He would spend his days shuttling around the polluted beaches of Shore Haven, the Stalinesque high rises of Co-op City, the once elegant Grand Concourse, the post-apocalyptic wasteland of the South Bronx, the tidy Jewish enclaves of Pelham Parkway and Riverdale.

Tony loved the excitement of the campaign, our aunt remembered, loved huddling over pizza, poll results, and position papers with seasoned political operatives in the Bronx trailer, loved meeting tough New York power brokers such as Roy Cohn and Stanley Friedman. But what he was most atttracted to was the energy of the streets. Abzug, a commanding character in trademark floppy hats, drew enthusiastic crowds at every campaign stop, from swimming clubs in luxury high-rises in Riverdale to bodegas beneath the elevated train tracks in the shadow of Yankee Stadium. She was a screamer, and Tony was often on the receiving end of her outbursts. Still, my aunt remembered, he worshiped Abzug. She lost her primary bid that September, but the experience had turned my brother into a political junkie.

When Tony returned to Performing Arts for his junior year, he discarded his jeans and black leather jackets and began wearing three-piece suits. His conversational focus shifted—from Pacino versus Hoffman to Carter versus Kennedy. His goal, he told his friends, was the Beltway, not Broadway. In the spring he announced his candidacy for Performing Arts' student body president, a position that, up to that time, few of his classmates took seriously. It was as if, one of his friends recalled, Tony had switched identities. It was as if, one said, he was telling everyone, "I'm separating from you. I'm not an actor anymore. I'm something more."

Nobody at Performing Arts had ever seen anything like it before—the intensity, the utter seriousness of purpose that he poured into his race for student body president. He campaigned from classroom to classroom, gave stump speeches, promised to institute a "Rock Day" once a week in the student cafeteria, breaking the disco stranglehold imposed by the school's dancers. His friends laughed at him, and called his behavior more of Tony's clowning around; then they too became caught up in the campaign. On the morning of the election, a half dozen of them stuffed the ballot boxes—without Tony's knowledge—and he won an easy victory. Soon afterward, Elvis Costello replaced the Bee Gees in the basement cafeteria on Tuesdays, prompting an angry walkout by the dancers.

* * *

By his senior year in high school, my brother had all but abandoned any interest in the theater. He talked of working on Capitol Hill as a congressional aide as soon as he graduated. He took his friends dancing at a post-campaign party for Bella Abzug at Studio 54, served on New York City mayor Edward Koch's student advisory council, ran the Manhattan campaign of a state assemblyman. Sixty miles away at Princeton, I didn't see Tony much in those days. But I remember how much I envied my brother's passions, the spirit with which he threw himself into every endeavor, the fire with which he could talk about everything—from the Bronx political machine to the method acting approach of Konstantin Stanislavsky. Envied too his friendships, which seemed to go to more profound levels than my own.

Marc Gatlin, an African American from the Harlem projects, was the friend to whom he felt closest. Marc was the star of the High School of Performing Arts senior class—a gangly jester who was always surrounded by admirers. He staged mock weddings for his friends in a Times Square pizza parlor, tearing up napkins and showering the young "marrieds" with the shreds. He led his classmates on romps through the subways, knocking on the loudspeaker during garbled announcements, shouting, "Say what? We can't hear you!" Although he grew up in Harlem, Marc was an ardent Reagan supporter, and he and my brother would debate politics for hours. Mostly, they were rambunctious teenagers. Once, in front of Performing Arts, Marc chased my brother into West Forty-sixth Street—and into the path of a moving car. Tony was knocked to the ground, suffering some scrapes and bruises. He and Marc laughed about the incident for months.

On a Saturday morning in the fall of 1977—the beginning of Tony's senior year—Marc and another classmate rode a train to Long Island to watch a friend perform in a school play. The classmate years later recounted how they chased each other with shopping carts around a supermarket, wandered into a synagogue and talked about God, lay in the grass in a public park and waited for the play to begin. At one point in the late afternoon, Marc noticed some teenagers who were running along a jogging path. "I wish I could do that," he said cryptically. Then he stood up, ran after them—and suddenly fell to the ground. A woman ran over from a nearby tennis court and performed mouth-to-mouth resuscitation on him. By then he was unconscious. An ambulance arrived a few minutes later, but Marc died on the way to the hospital. He was seventeen years old.

His friends were stunned, disbelieving. But looking back years later, several of them recalled that there had been warnings. Marc had been cold all the time, wore a down parka even during the New York summer. He was always rubbing baby oil into his skin, explaining that he needed to improve his circulation. He poured huge amounts of sugar into his Coke, explaining that he needed it "for energy." He complained of shortness of breath and, on at least one occasion, told friends he expected to die young. But nobody had known the truth: Marc had sickle cell anemia and an enlarged heart. His early death had been foreordained.

Hundreds of grief-stricken students, teachers, and relatives attended the service at the Frank E. Campbell Funeral Home on Madison Avenue. Afterward, Marc's classmates, including my brother, gathered at a friend's apartment to mourn. Tony seemed to take Marc's death the hardest of all of them, a friend recalled years later. He was sobbing, distraught, inconsolable. After Marc's death the clique was never quite the same. Many had grown up in broken and dysfunctional households, and their tight-knit group had functioned as a surrogate family—a magic circle. Marc had been the most nurturing of all of them. Now the magic circle had been broken.

WHEN I RETURNED TO MONSEY FOR A THIRD visit later in the winter, I came with a more specific agenda. I wanted to find out more about the mysterious Hasidic rabbi that my mother had mentioned to me in Africa. I was becoming increasingly aware of my brother's affinity throughout his life for charismatic figures—gurus—some benign, others more questionable. I had heard fragmented accounts about my brother's most recent infatuation: how the rabbi had been convicted of kidnapping; how my brother had visited him in prison; and how the relationship had come between him and his wife.

During my previous stay in Monsey I thought I sensed the rabbi's presence hanging over the house, in the tension that sometimes permeated conversations between my brother and Ahuva, in the deepening fervor that infected my brother's prayers and attitudes. His physical appearance—the long black overcoat, the unkempt beard, the peyyes—also reflected a more austere Hasidic influence that had not characterized him when I had visited him in

Monsey before going to Africa. So far I had not found the opportunity to raise the subject.

But shortly after I arrived for my third stay, my brother and I drove to the Monsey Glatt Kosher Market to buy some ice cream for the children. On the road, I asked him about the rabbi. He immediately warned me that anything he said was not to be brought up around his wife and children. But yes, he conceded as we parked the car in the market's lot, the rabbi was a great man, a tsaddik, a righteous individual. They had met four years earlier, my brother said, after a Hasidic neighbor phoned and told him that he had encountered someone whom Tuvia might like to get to know.

"His name is Rabbi Shlomo Helbrans," the neighbor said.

"I've never heard of him," my brother said.

The rabbi, it turned out, was a well-known figure among New York's Hasidim—and Brooklyn criminal prosecutors. Some time earlier, Israeli emigres living in Paramus, New Jersey, had sent their twelve-year-old son to the rabbi's yeshiva for bar mitzvah lessons. Hannah Fhima and her husband were not religious Jews, but they had felt comfortable with the Hebrew-speaking, Israeli rabbi. One week later, however, the boy, Shai Fhima, began wearing Hasidic garb. When Fhima's mother brought him home, he escaped and made his way back to the yeshiva in Borough Park, Brooklyn. In April 1992, after a two-month tug-of-war with Rabbi Helbrans, the boy's mother went to pick up her son at the home of an ultra-Orthodox associate of the rabbi's in Monsey. The boy had vanished, and neither Helbrans nor the associate claimed to have any idea where he had gone.

Shai Fhima's mother did not believe them; she went to the police. Two months later, with her son still missing, a federal grand jury was convened, and the United States attorney in Brooklyn and the FBI began an investigation into the boy's disappearance. On a Friday morning in February 1993, a team of FBI agents, New York state troopers, and city detectives stormed the rabbi's home in Monsey and took Helbrans and his wife, Malka, in handcuffs to the Brooklyn House of Detention. Released on $250,000 bond, Helbrans was later indicted on charges of kidnapping and conspiracy. The main evidence against him, which had emerged during nine months of grand jury testimony, consisted of notes and recordings suggesting that he had known all along where Shai Fhima was being hidden, and that he had offered $60,000 cash to Fhima's mother in return for permanent custody of the boy.

My brother first visited Shlomo Helbrans at his attorney's office in midtown Manhattan. His Hasidic neighbor had recommended him to the attorney as someone who could translate legal documents into Yiddish for the rabbi's benefit. Helbrans, who called himself the Lev Tohor Rov (Rabbi Pure of Heart), had uneven teeth and a tendency to stammer—like Moses—and he drew my brother close with a low, hoarse voice that sometimes shrank to a whisper. They talked about the details of the case—a clear example, the rabbi said, of the hostility of the secular world toward Orthodox religious belief—and then turned their attentions to the Torah and the ways of serving Hashem.

The discussions continued over the next few months whenever my brother would drive the rabbi home to Monsey from the attorney's Midtown office. "Rebbe, can I ask you a question?" he would begin. Then the Lev Tohor Rov would launch into a lecture about various facets of halacha, or Jewish law, and Jewish thought: modesty, controlling anger, the darkness of secular society, laziness, the hidden meanings of words in the Torah. Once they drove to Washington, D.C., for a meeting with lawyers, and as the Lev Tohor Rov and a Hasidic study companion argued over fine points in the Gemorah, my brother listened, rapt, for six hours, astonished that a man barely thirty years old could possess such insight into the complexities of Jewish life.

At the heart of the Lev Tohor Rov's philosophy was the concept of *upgegebenkeit*—the emotional surrender of the self to the love of God. It was an idea first propounded by the Baal Shem Tov, the Polish rabbi who founded Hasidism in the eighteenth century as a reaction against the rationalist tradition that then dominated the Jewish world. The Baal Shem Tov preached to poor Jews in the shtetls that singing, dancing, and davening—the fervent bowing at the waist that signals devotion—were as important as studying the Talmud in bringing a person close to the Almighty. God was everywhere, he said, and a Jew must infuse each part of his day—from eating to sexual relations—with absolute reverence and awe and joy.

The Lev Tohor Rov took the Baal Shem Tov's teachings to a new level of intensity. A Jew must devote himself to God at every moment with every fiber, every molecule of his being, he warned my brother, or "when he passes into the next world, he's going to discover that Hashem's love for him was so much greater than he imagined that he's going to hide his head in shame." The epitome of such selflessness was Abraham, who was willing to sacrifice his own son, Isaac, to express his love for the Almighty. Worshiping God properly required a willingness to sacrifice the things one loved most, the rabbi said. A person might even have to separate himself from his wife, his family, *chas v'sholem*—God forbid—if they should put up obstacles to his wholehearted devotion. "Tuvia, your Jewish engines are running at only sixty percent capacity," Helbrans told my brother. "With the Hasidic way of life, you can rev those engines up to ninety, one hundred percent."

The route to pure devotion was difficult, he said. Tuvia needed to cleanse his nashama thoroughly of what Helbrans called "the mud of secular culture" and "goyish philosophy." The Enlightenment, when notions of humanism and evolution caused man to question his relationship to God, had been the undoing of the Jewish people, Helbrans said. Many Jews were lured out of their ghettos. They became skeptics, materialists, and turned away from the Almighty. In the late twentieth century, and especially in the United States, those secular temptations were more powerful than ever.

There were steps someone like my brother could take. A daily or twice daily mikvah would help him to guard his purity, coating his body—or *guf*—with a protective ointment of holy water. Reading the Gemorah intensively—nine hours, ten hours per day—would help him penetrate deeply into the foundations of *amuna*, or faith. Intense davening would allow him to blot out all thoughts of trivial matters like work and money and send his heart soaring with love for God. One form of davening favored by the rabbi was called *stalin karlin*: raising the voice as high as possible, screaming one's love of Hashem, obliterating all distracting ideas and arousing the emotions to their highest levels. The other method was called *shuckling*—shaking the body violently in all directions as one chanted prayers.

Our mother, who was still visiting Monsey once every three months, began to notice a new fervor in her son around this time, she told me, and a growing hostility toward non-Jewish influence. The previous year she and Ahuva had taken the children shopping at Barnes and Noble, brought home Curious George and Berenstain Bears paperbacks, and encountered no objections from my brother. But now when she arrived at my brother's home bearing a $25 Barnes and Noble gift certificate, he confronted her.

"I don't want you buying books for the children—ever again," he said.

Our mother stared at him, dumbstruck. She found it difficult to comprehend her son's antipathy toward seemingly harmless animal stories.

Ahuva had also watched her husband's transformation with concern, she told me one evening at the house. Until he met the Lev Tohor Rov, he had considered himself a *misnoggid*—a type of Litvisher Jew who was opposed to the Hasidim. In the eighteenth century, the original misnoggidim had recoiled from the Hasidim's unchecked expressions of emotion. They disparaged them as "madmen"—and their modern-day counterparts retained much of that hostility. Indeed, for most of their marriage, Ahuva said, she had been more attracted to the Hasidic way of life than my brother. In the late 1980s Ahuva had become friendly with a Hasidic teacher at her ultra-Orthodox kindergarten for girls, and had received an invitation to spend Shabbos in New Square. She had to drag her husband with her. The Hasidim, he said, spent too much of their lives praying and dancing, and bathing in the mikvah, instead of studying the Talmud.

But now under Helbrans's influence, my brother began to distance himself from fellow Litvisher Jews, such as Rabbi Rosenman. His physical appearance, even his accent changed. He seemed to be reinventing himself—just as he had recreated himself as an actor, a politician, and a Torah Jew. He grew out his beard and his peyyes, and began to wear the *rekel*, an ankle-length black overcoat preferred by Hasidim. He threw himself into the study of Yiddish. He davened at all hours, with greater intensity. He became obsessed with the mikvah, bathing two, sometimes three times a day.

Politically he changed as well. Once a passionate Zionist, he now echoed the Lev Tohor Rov's venomous hostility toward the state of Israel. Helbrans and certain other Hasidic leaders maintain that the Torah strictly forbids the Jews from establishing a state in the holy land until the Messiah appears on earth and leads them to Zion. My brother now held that "Only God can proclaim an end to the exile," and blamed the Zionists for delaying the arrival of the Messiah by contravening God's law. He referred to Israeli independence day as Yom hashmutz—the dirty day. The Zionists had compounded their sins against God, he said, by bringing millions of observant Jewish immigrants to the holy land and tearing them from their heritage. Later, he would rejoice along with the Lev Tohor Rov when a right-wing Jewish assassin murdered Israeli Prime Minister Yitzhak Rabin. The killer had not shot Rabin for the "right" reasons, he said— the Jews should give back all their land to the Arabs, as far as he was concerned—but the end result was worth celebrating all the same.

Soon he began trying to sweep his family into the Hasidic world as well. He put pressure on Ahuva to enroll their sons in a Hasidic yeshiva. There, boys spoke nothing but Yiddish and all wore long, braided peyyes. They prayed, studied, ate, and breathed yiddishkeit. There were no bicycles, no baseball, no games, no English, no mixing with girls, no interaction with the outside world. Ahuva would have none of it. She appreciated the beauty of *chasidis*—the Hasidic way of life—and had many Hasidic friends. But she would not accept it for her children. If the boys talked about baseball or played a little street hockey in Manny Weldler Park, she would not object, she told my brother.

Ahuva, I was coming to realize, was a very different personality from her husband. If my brother had always seemed fraught with inner torment, self doubt, and unbridled passion, Ahuva seemed to live her life on a much more even keel. Even her journey into ultra-Orthodoxy had been largely free of the angst of my brother's dramatic reinvention. For one thing, she told me, she had always believed in God—it had just taken her a while to figure out which

God to believe in. Her great-great-grandmother was an observant Jew from Austria, but Ahuva's great-grandmother had abandoned Judaism. Ahuva, born Andrea, grew up with only a vague knowledge of her Jewish roots. Raised in Queens and Westchester as an Episcopalian, she attended church on Sundays, wrote "Dear God" letters in her diary from the age of nine—when her parents divorced—and later taught Baptist Sunday school in a church in rural Tennessee.

But at sixteen, after years of shuttling between her Catholic mother and her Episcopalian father, she moved in with her maternal grandmother in Kew Gardens, Queens, and began exploring her Jewish roots. She watched the ultra-Orthodox stroll to synagogue in her neighborhood with fascination. She began wearing a star of David, read Jewish history at the local library, lit candles on Friday nights, read prayers at Rosh Hashonah, and tried to keep kosher, although she wasn't quite sure about the rules. She would place macaroni and cheese on one plate and hamburger on another, and eat them simultaneously using separate utensils. "What are you doing?" her grandmother asked her one night.

"I'm separating meat and milk," she told her grandmother, who, dimly recalling the Jewish rituals of her childhood, gently explained that the foods were not meant to be eaten together.

At seventeen, she joined an Orthodox shul. At Queens College, she wore long skirts and blouses that covered her arms to the wrists, joined Jewish youth organizations such as Hillel, and sang Hebrew songs with guitar-playing rabbis on Saturday nights. At nineteen, she dropped out of college and entered Netzer Yisroel, the only girls' yeshiva in Monsey. Her friends and parents thought she was crazy. Other women in her class soon dropped out, uncomfortable with the subservience of women to men in the Orthodox world. But Ahuva never experienced a moment's doubt.

Perhaps, Ahuva mused, the fact that my brother had come into Orthodox Judaism later in life compelled him to try that much harder to purify his soul. Perhaps he had to deny the secular world utterly in order to free himself of its residual temptations. Perhaps, I thought, by identifying himself so closely with the divine he could fill some psychic vacuum within himself. Whatever the reasons, my brother's movement to the radical fringe of ultra-Orthodox Judaism had a familiar ring to it. In politics, acting, in every one of his passions, he seemed driven to embrace extremes. There was a hunger for perfection, a restless spirit, a deep-seated dissatisfaction with himself that seemed to propel him forward until he had nowhere left to go. My brother seemed to lack the braking mechanisms that hold most people back, that alert them to the loss of balance in their lives. In his infatuation with Shlomo Helbrans, he seemed to be plunging headlong into a bottomless abyss.

As my brother's commitment to Helbrans deepened, he began raising money for the rabbi's legal fund, laying out his case to other rabbis in ultra-Orthodox shuls across New York and New Jersey. The rabbis would make an appeal before their congregations and pass around collection boxes. My brother obtained private audiences with the highly respected Viznitz rebbe in Monsey, the Skvira rebbe in New Square, and the Satmar rebbe in Monroe, New York—powerful spiritual leaders who could raise $60,000 with a single request in shul. The money poured in—from Borough Park, Monsey, Monroe, Antwerp, Jerusalem— $300,000 in a few months. Although he lacked even an undergraduate degree, my brother became the Lev Tohor Rov's unofficial legal adviser—helping to craft a plea-bargain agreement with the Brooklyn district attorney that collapsed at the last minute.

The failed plea bargain set the stage for one of the most theatrical and emotional events of recent years in the Brooklyn courts. Hundreds of Hasidic followers of the Lev Tohor Rov packed the courtroom benches during his six-week kidnapping trial in Brooklyn Supreme Court, which began on October 10, 1994. The rabbi's lawyers argued that the boy was escaping from a violent stepfather and a dysfunctional mother, and that he was old enough to make his own decisions. Shai Fhima took the witness stand, clad in Hasidic garb, to testify that he had voluntarily joined Helbrans's sect. The prosecution said Helbrans had manipulated the boy and organized a Hasidic underground railroad in Monsey, and France, to hide him from his family for more than two years.

Except for one brief visit, my brother stayed away from the courthouse. He had been in touch with the protectors of Shai Fhima during his disappearance, he told me, and was afraid that his presence in the courtroom might draw the attention of the prosecutors, who were still seeking links between Helbrans and those who had hidden the boy. But he visited Helbrans during the trial at the apartment the rabbi had leased in the Sea Gate neighborhood of Brooklyn, and stayed beside him the night before the jury returned its verdict. Helbrans, my brother recalled, was calm and defiant as he waited to discover his fate. "They think they're just going up against Shlomo Helbrans," he said. "But I'm just the tip of the iceberg. The Yiddin have a depth that can sink the *Titanic*." Although his attorneys had repeatedly assured him that he was going home, the rabbi was expecting the worst.

Dozens of Hasidim prayed in the hallway of the courthouse while the jury deliberated on November 16. My brother held vigil with other supporters at the home of the Satmar rebbe in

Williamsburg. After five hours the jury filed back into the court-room somberly and announced its verdict: guilty of kidnapping, guilty of conspiracy. Some Hasidim wailed; Helbrans stared grimly at the defense table. Malka Helbrans collapsed as her husband was led away to Rikers Island to await sentencing. Others in the courtroom rejoiced. "I lost my son because of Rabbi Helbrans, and I finally see justice," Hanna Fhima told reporters. "He got what he deserves."

Judge Thaddeus Owens sentenced Helbrans to four to twelve years at Greenhaven Correctional Facility, a maximum-security penitentiary for violent offenders in upstate New York. The rabbi remained unrepentant. "Your Honor," Helbrans said before he was led away in handcuffs, "the charge that Orthodox rabbis abduct children is as accurate as the blood libel in the name of which Jews were slaughtered throughout the ages, as if Jews avail themselves of Christian blood for Passover. I will march to prison with the same faith that my fathers and fore-fathers displayed when they walked to their deaths. I will proudly proclaim the prayer of God's Oneness. 'Hear Israel, God is our Lord, God is One.' "

Now, nearly four years later, Shlomo Helbrans was back in Monsey, living and teaching in the Lev Tohor yeshiva just a few blocks from my brother's home. One night during my third visit I asked my brother if he would take me for an audience with the rabbi. He told me that he couldn't. Ahuva had forced him to resign from his job as an administrator at the Lev Tohor yeshiva the previous December and had forbidden him ever to return. But I persuaded him to telephone the Lev Tohor Rov on my behalf—and try to set up a one-on-one meeting.

The next day he told me that the rabbi had agreed to see me "if you're willing to make a serious commitment."

"What does he mean, 'serious'?"

"You have to be willing to spend three days and nights at the yeshiva."

I hesitated. Three days and nights seemed a little more time than I was willing to give up. More phone calls passed back and forth. At last we received a message. The Lev Tohor Rov would see me immediately, with no conditions attached.

A half hour later, I parked my brother's car in a deserted lot behind the Viznitz girls' yeshiva on School Terrace, as my brother had instructed, and followed a muddy trail through a copse of maple trees. As I approached the house, I began to hear a strange sound, a blood-curdling howl not unlike the baying of a pack of wolves. At the end of a long gravel driveway loomed a large red-brick home with a white-colonnaded portico. The cries, it now became clear, were coming from the basement. I walked around to the back of the house and down a flight of stone stairs. Pushing open the door, I stepped into a low-ceilinged library lined with leather-bound prayer books. Right before my eyes, twenty Hasidim were davening before a make-shift holy Ark. They were screaming, wailing, trembling, and bending at the waist at what seemed like machine-gun speed. They ranged from white-bearded geriatrics to beardless teenagers, although most appeared to be in their twenties and thirties. I watched them davening for about ten minutes. Then the prayers ended, and two of the Hasidim approached me.

"Shalom aleichem, shalom aleichem," they cried. "You're Tuvia's brother?"

I nodded. "Come and join us," one beckoned. The Hasidim grabbed my hands, and we linked up with the rest of the minyan, or prayer group, who had begun dancing around a large study table, chanting a wordless melody. I circled the room about two dozen times, until I began to feel dizzy, and sat down in a corner.

When the dance ended, a half dozen Hasidim crowded around me. How was Tuvia? they asked. Why couldn't he sneak away and join me tonight? Everybody knew about the ban on my brother's visits here. My brother had been a big macher—a bigshot—in the rabbi's little world. He had served as legal adviser, yeshiva administator, star pupil, gatekeeper to the press, and fund-raiser. His loss was deeply felt, and I detected some resentment toward his wife for forcing him to leave. "These American ladies," one of the Hasidim muttered, "are very stubborn people."

The Lev Tohor Rov's acolytes were ex-Israeli soldiers, with a few Russian baal tshuvas sprinkled into the mix. Uriel Yosef Goldman, a strapping, thirtyish Hasid who had replaced my brother as administrator, was, I was startled to discover, the nephew of an Israeli air force general. Ten years ago, he told me as I waited for my audience with the rabbi, he was dodging the stones of Palestinian demonstrators in Hebron, dreaming of a career as a professional soldier. "Politically," he said in lightly accented English, "I was further to the right than Likud." Then, in 1989, his brother brought him to hear Helbrans speak at a kibbutz on the West Bank. At the height of the *intifada*, the young rabbi preached an unexpected message: the Zionist entity was a sin against the Torah. "It was the opposite of everything I ever thought about Israel," Goldman told me. "But I couldn't get his words out of my head."

Goldman attended more lectures at the rabbi's small yeshiva in Jerusalem. By that time the Lev Tohor Rov was being dogged by allegations that he had isolated students from their families and "brainwashed" them into becoming Hasidic. An angry mob attacked his wife on the street. Just before the start of the Persian Gulf War, Helbrans, his wife, and children—and a few dozen followers, including Goldman, left Israel, settling in Borough Park. "When I arrived in Brooklyn, I was dressed just like you—Nikes, Levi's, a flannel shirt, a knapsack on my back," Goldman said. Soon he grew peyyes and adopted Hasidic dress.

Goldman lived in Monsey now with his wife and four children, spending his days praying and studying Torah with the rabbi.

The Lev Tohor Rov's private secretary, known as a *gabbai*, entered the basement from an interior stairwell. With his ankle-length black robe, wispy beard and mustache, and almond-shaped eyes, he looked like a servant to a Chinese emperor. He nodded at me, then led me silently upstairs to a book-lined anteroom that adjoined the rabbi's study. A pale woman dressed in a brown frock and scarf—the Lev Tohor Rov's wife, Malka—fled into the kitchen as we passed. The odors of sour milk and beef stew wafted through the austere hallway.

The gabbai opened the door. Shlomo Helbrans sat, as still and alert as a lizard on a rock, in a red-leather armchair at the head of a table covered with white linen. Tightly coiled peyyes framed his wide bearded face, and he peered through a pair of steel-framed spectacles. A richly brocaded turquoise gown draped his large, portly body. Silver candelabra, an enamel washbasin and chalice, and a leather-bound Pentateuch, the five books of Moses, were arrayed on a washstand at his side.

"Welcome, Yehoshua," he rasped in a thick Hebrew accent. He apologized for his poor English and studied me through his heavy lenses. I cleared my throat and began to introduce myself.

"My brother has spoken highly of you," I said, "and I—"

Helbrans held up his hand. He smiled, exposing a set of crooked yellow teeth. "Sit down," he said. "Sit." He spoke with a lisp—"Thit down. Thit." I obeyed. He studied me a little longer. His eyes seemed to bore into me, and I shifted about uncomfortably.

"I have one question for you, Y-Yehoshua," he said with a slight stutter. "W—what is your purpose in life?"

"My purpose in life?"

Helbrans nodded. "I asked this to other inmates when I was in jail. Everybody had a different answer. So now I say to you again, 'What is your purpose in life?'"

I wasn't sure what he was fishing for. "Nobody really knows the answer to that question," I said. "To live a moral life, I guess, to find one's talent and excel in it, to—"

"All right. What is your definition of religious truth?"

Here I felt more confident. "I don't think there is one 'truth,'" I said. "All religions share similar values about morality and God. The key is tolerance, I think, accepting that all religions stem from a universal human impulse toward the divine, to make sense of the unknowable."

Helbrans flashed me a patronizing smile. "That's very pleasant, very well argued, very Western, very—American, Yehoshua," the Lev Tohor Rov said. "Unfortunately, it has no basis in truth. What if I could prove to you that I had the truth? Would you be willing to change your life?"

"Change my life?"

"If I could prove to you beyond any scientific doubt that the Almighty gave the Torah to Moshe Rebbenu on Mount Sinai, would you accept it and change your life—today?"

I felt uneasy. "You're a charismatic man," I told him. "You're a very able debater. You're articulate, convincing—"

"And," Helbrans said with a flourish, "I'm a kidnapper."

I was unsure how to react to his admission. We both laughed.

"I'm not sure I can hold my own against you," I admitted. "So if you ask me to sign on the dotted line, I'm not going to."

The Lev Tohor Rov laughed again.

Shlomo Helbrans told me that he had grown up in Jerusalem as the son of nonreligious Jews. "My first step was sitting alone, reading the Torah," he told me. "I was thirteen years old, the same age as Shai Fhima. Then I met a young boy, a few years older than me. Ten days I was with him day and night." Helbrans moistened his lips with a sip of water. His voice grew raspier, his lisp thickened, and his stutter worsened the more he talked. "My parents didn't know. I took my swimming trunks and towel and said, 'I'm going out to the pool.' After ten days like this I came home to my parents and said, 'I've decided to become religious.' They shrieked—it was just like Shai's parents. My father went after this kid and beat him on the street. 'Your son came after me!' the kid protested. 'When people come to me to discuss things, what am I supposed to do?' "

It was a curious parallel, Helbrans said, to find himself arrested for doing much the same thing, for helping to show another Jew the way to religious truth. When they took him to prison, he said, his belief was confirmed—that the Jews are the most hated race on earth: "When I was in jail, all of the thieves, the murderers, the worst of the worst, I heard maybe one hundred times a day, 'Don't jew me, man, don't you be jewing me, man.' You know how many gentiles believe stories about Jews drinking blood? In jail, everybody. They told me, 'It's a hundred percent certain.' "

"Did you argue with them?"

"We had . . . discussions. If somebody was angry at you, they'd cut your face, so I stayed away from arguments. Especially with the Muslims. Sixty percent of the blacks became Muslims in jail—the strongest power group inside the prison. Some of them were poisonous—particularly the preachers. Some were serious people."

"Did you mix with these Muslims?"

"They put me at first in the protected section, because the jail supervisor was one hundred percent convinced that if I went into the general population I would be cut in two minutes."

"Because you were a Jew?"

"Because I was a Hasidic Jew, a famous rabbi, and because I received privileges to pray and eat good kosher food. Many of the prisoners are animals—murderers, rapists. But 'protective custody' meant being alone in a box—with no connection to the other Jews there. I screamed that I wanted to go out. They made me wait a few weeks just to decide if I was serious or not. They said, 'Rabbi, after two minutes you're going to be back in here, with a knife sticking out of you. Hashem won't help you.' But when they let me out of solitary, a miracle happened. I got respect. The toughest men in the prison, black Muslims, surrounded me. 'This is my main man, don't touch the rabbi!' they said. To me it meant that Hashem was saying, 'I don't want to punish you any more than that you should be in here.'"

"You believe that Hashem wanted you to suffer?"

He smiled. "Of course."

"Why?"

"Because of my sins. I have very, very many."

"If he makes you suffer, what is he going to do to somebody like me?"

The rabbi laughed. "Now you know why I worry about you, Yehoshua," he said.

There was a sharp rap on the door. A small boy—Helbrans's son—brought in teacups, a teapot, and a plate of chocolate wafers. He laid the tray on the table without making eye contact with me, turned, and scurried out of the room. "We eat something now," Helbrans said. "But first we wash." The rabbi poured water from the enamel basin three times over each of his hands with the chalice, muttered the blessing, and motioned for me to follow suit. I recited the Hebrew confidently—by now I had performed the ritual countless times at my brother's home— and Helbrans nodded in approval.

God had put him through many tests in prison, Helbrans told me, to see if he would stand by his faith. The prison authorities demanded that Helbrans shave his beard and take off his yarmulke. He threatened to starve himself to death if forced to comply. He would not eat the kosher food provided to Jewish prisoners, claiming that he couldn't be certain of its origins. For the first three weeks he subsisted on oranges and occasional plates of kugel prepared by a sympathetic Jewish cook in the prison kitchen—until the warden relented and permitted him weekly deliveries of kosher food from Monsey, a maximum of thirty pounds a month.

One day during recreation time, the guards refused to allow the rabbi to leave the yard to use the toilet. The Torah forbids holding in one's bodily functions, so the rebbe urinated in a corner of the yard. Prison authorities clapped him into "the box"—a windowless six-foot-by-six-foot isolation cell—for ten straight days.

Against my expectations, I was beginning to like the Lev Tohor Rov. I had been anticipating a stern ascetic; instead I was encountering an engaging raconteur with a surprising connection to the outside world. We had been talking for more than an hour, and I was growing weary. I told the Lev Tohor Rov that I would return on my next trip to Monsey. Helbrans shrugged. "Yehoshua, it's your life," he croaked. His voice had almost faded away. "I just try to bring you the message, 'Hurry.' You're living in Theresienstadt."

"Theresienstadt?"

"Theresienstadt, the concentration camp in Nazi Germany." It had been, the Lev Tohor Rov explained, a Nazi propaganda tool used to persuade the outside world that Germany's Jews were all being treated well. One day, Helbrans said, a man came to the fence and whispered to the Jews inside: "Get out! Run for your lives!" But the Jews were enjoying themselves—listening to violin concertos, savoring the hearty food. "Go away, you fool," they told him. Then one day the Nazis closed the camp and shipped them all to Auschwitz. Theresienstadt, Helbrans said with a crooked-toothed smile, was the secular world. And unless I left the secular world in a hurry and embraced Judaism, I might be condemned to a place more terrible than Auschwitz.

"Hurry, Yehoshua. Hurry," the Lev Tohor Rov told me as I rose from my chair.

"I'll be back," I told the rabbi.

"I'll try to help you. But remember: time is running out."

I walked silently down the driveway toward the car, listening to the screech of owls in the surrounding woods and the crunching of gravel beneath my feet. The cool night air revived me. My audience with the rabbi had been unsettling. There was something deeply seductive about him. I felt that I understood how someone young and impressionable—someone such as Shai Fhima—could find himself drawn under his spell so quickly. My brother, too, had always been easy prey to talkers, charismatics who exuded certainty. I felt relieved to be out of the Lev Tohor Rov's domain.

"You can tell he's a genius, can't you?" asked my brother later that night.

"He makes me nervous."

"He's not asking you to sign up for life. He understands that you're too weak. You're still too attached to the other parts of your life."

A half dozen times during the rabbi's two years in prison, my brother told me that night, he drove two hours north to visit him at Greenhaven Correctional Facility, a bleak fortress surrounded by fifty-foot walls, and, later, a second prison in New York State. Prison guards carrying machine guns kept watch from high concrete towers. Clad in a green prison-issue smock and a green cap over his yarmulke, the Lev Tohor Rov would shuffle into the smoke-filled visitors lounge and spend an hour huddled with his protégé, lecturing him about faith, the mitzvahs, the Torah, over the din of other inmates. On one visit a fight broke out between guards and a prisoner in the next room. My brother closed the window between the rooms, but they could still hear the curses, the crash of furniture, the cries and thuds of fists against flesh. Rabbi Helbrans called such episodes part of his "trial by God."

After months of negotiation, the rabbi won the right to observe Jewish festivals behind the prison walls. Each *rosh chodesh*, the first day of the Jewish lunar month, prison guards escorted the rabbi outside at night to pray and dance beneath the new moon.

For the eight-day October holiday known as Sukkos, the warden even allowed him to dwell in a *sukkah*—a hut that symbolizes the clouds of glory that protected the Jews during their wanderings in the Sinai Desert—in an isolated part of the prison courtyard. As my brother watched, guards stretched sheets of transparent plastic over a metal frame and topped the structure with a roof of corn stalks harvested from fields outside the prison walls. Then my brother joined a dozen Jewish inmates, and an African American convict contemplating conversion to Judaism, who had gathered in the makeshift tabernacle. Draped in a ceremonial white gown and a white yarmulke, the rebbe led the celebrants in a three-hour ritual of singing, dancing, and prayer. The guards looked on, amazed.

I tried to picture the scene: the bare concrete walls of the courtyard, a sliver of sky, my brother and his rabbi wailing Hebrew incantations in their plastic-walled hut under the watchful eyes of the prison screws. My mind reeled from the thought of it. My brother's journey into religious zealotry, I thought, had surely reached the end of the road here in this bleak fortress filled with rapists and murderers. But I was wrong.

. . .

Ahuva had watched it all unfolding with a growing sense of helplessness. The rabbi's "religion" was all about mind control, not the love of God, she told me as I sat with her in the kitchen, listening to the strange story of my brother's indoctrination from her perspective. Shlomo Helbrans had placed himself above the Torah, she believed, above tsaddikim such as the Viznitz rebbe, who had ascended to his lofty station through decades of scholarship and a noble lineage. She had been alarmed by the changes in my brother's behavior, she told me, horrified by the rabbi's strengthening hold on him. During the trial Ahuva had been pregnant with her second daughter—her fifth child—and her husband was spending almost all his days and nights in Brooklyn, raising money for the rabbi's appeal—as a volunteer. Ahuva was running her kindergarten eight hours a day while taking care of her own five children and trying single-handedly to keep the house from falling apart. Depressed, exhausted, she sought counseling from Monsey's rabbis, but they could offer her little advice.

The nightmare deepened. His jail sentence reduced on appeal, the Lev Tohor Rov returned to Monsey, thin and sick, after exactly two years behind bars. My brother was there to welcome him. Soon he began davening and learning Torah at the rabbi's side around the clock, managing the Lev Tohor Yeshiva, huddling with architects day after day discussing plans for a mikvah in the basement. He was spending less and less time at home. On Yom Kippur, 1997, he remained in Helbrans' synagogue alone until five o'clock in the morning. The crisis reached a climax at Simchas Torah, the last of the High Holy Days. The children went with their father to pray that morning; by nightfall there was still no sign of them. That night Ahuva dashed around Monsey in a panic, bursting into the homes of friends, crying, "Have you seen my children?" My brother returned with them early the next morning. He had taken them to watch the Lev Tohor Rov dance with the Torah at his yeshiva all night long and not bothered to inform Ahuva of their whereabouts.

After that, she needed to escape, she told me. She left her youngest children in the custody of neighbors in Monsey, then retreated to her mother's cottage in Lakewood, New Jersey, to collect her thoughts. She left my brother with their two oldest boys—and a warning that he must cut off all contact with the Lev Tohor Rov. But my brother seemed to be oblivious. The rabbi's visa had lapsed while he was in prison—he was still an Israeli citizen—and he now faced the possibility of deportation. His old lawyers had broken off their relationship with him following a financial dispute, and Helbrans needed new legal representation in a hurry. My brother approached Rabbi Meisels and begged him for help. He had been close to Meisels, but his deepening infatuation with the Lev Tohor Rov had driven them apart.

"Could you take care of the boys after school?" he asked.

"Now you're coming and talking to me?" Meisels snapped. "You practically spit at me before."

"I'm desperate," he said. "I'm trying to get the rabbi a new lawyer."

"You'd better get two lawyers," Meisels replied. "One for the rabbi and one for you, because if you don't stop making life miserable for your family, you might not get back into your house."

My brother would not talk much about this chapter of his life, but it was easy for me to picture him as a father left in a disintegrating house, forced suddenly to feed and clothe his sons and send them off to school, forced to manage his financial affairs and devote time to the quotidian details of life. It had been years, I knew, since he had picked up a hammer or a screwdriver, changed a lightbulb, hung a curtain, sewed a button on a shirt.

It had been years since he had dwelled alone, or even been separated for more than one day from his wife. Losing Ahuva, even briefly, was undoubtedly a terrible shock.

From her refuge in Lakewood, Ahuva begged Meisels and other rabbis to intervene for her, she told me. Somehow, this time he was more susceptible to their influence. They informed my brother that he was in danger of losing his *mishpocha,* his wife and children, for good. Had he forgotten that the most important *mitzvah* for a Jew was to strive for *shalom bayyes*—family harmony? Suddenly, as Ahuva told me this story, I realized why the house had been empty and in such disrepair that late November afternoon when I visited my brother. Ahuva had moved out—and he had been too pained to tell me the truth.

By the time Ahuva and I spoke about Helbrans in her kitchen, my brother had been out of the yeshiva for three months. Life had marginally improved. But the Lev Tohor Rov's influence remained powerful. My brother was still jobless, soaking regularly in the mikvah, studying Talmud eight hours a day, davening at all hours, arguing with Ahuva about the kids' education. Ahuva's mother had been pressing her to draw the line. "You're raising the children, you're sewing, you're working. He doesn't earn a living. He's copping out," she said. But Ahuva was temporarily satisfied, she said, merely to have her husband back. "I have to accept Tuvia as he is," she told me. I wondered how long she would feel that way.

RUMMAGING THROUGH A CARDBOARD BOX stashed deep in a closet in my father's apartment, looking for clues to my brother's transformation, I stumbled upon his high school yearbook from the class of 1978. Folded up inside it was a short story that he had written shortly before he graduated. A thinly veiled work about our half sister Allison, the narrative laid bare some of the emotions that my brother had always kept hidden from me during that period. Reading his words, I began to understand for the first time the bond that he had shared with her, and the intense pain he must have felt after the loss.

She was born in April 1975, during the worst days of the Lucky Luciano scandal. Our father and Arlene had been left without medical insurance, and they were forced to borrow the money to pay for the birth. My brother and I both visited Arlene and her new daughter at Mount Sinai Hospital, on a warm spring morning, sharing our father's and stepmother's delight in the tiny creature who had entered their lives. "She lay in the hospital nursery, emitting a glow which betrayed her delight at being alive,"

Tony wrote. "Every family thinks its child is unique, but there was something special about this one—something which created within all a sense of serenity. . . . A love emerged between her and her brother which was rare and special."

Born into a situation of financial deprivation, Allison wore hand-me-downs from cousins and played with empty milk cartons instead of toys. But she was an ebullient, extroverted baby, and I don't believe that she ever felt deprived. Arlene began to wind down her theatrical career after Allison's birth and soon became a full-time mother. During the winter she would take her daughter to play in the snow in Central Park, and they would admire the polar bears in the Central Park Zoo. Early on, she exposed her daughter to the music of Mary Martin's *Peter Pan*, Leonard Bernstein's *Peter and the Wolf*, and the *Nutcracker Suite*. Allison was a source of joy for my father and his wife—the one bright spot in an otherwise grim period of their lives.

Then, one Wednesday morning at the beginning of spring in New York, just after Allison's second birthday, they noticed that her eyes were a little swollen and puffy. Both of them were chronic sinus sufferers, and they assumed that she had inherited their condition. But the swelling worsened—alarmingly. By Saturday morning their daughter's eyes were swollen shut, barely slits, their eyelashes invisible. Her whole face was grotesquely bloated, her stomach distended, her arms soft and puffy. Arlene, in a panic, marched into the pediatrician's office with her daughter. The doctor took one look, then ordered a urine specimen. The next morning, he had Allison admitted to Mount Sinai Hospital. "It looks like childhood nephrosis," he said.

The words sounded grim, lethal, when our father called me at Princeton University to tell me the diagnosis. He and Arlene had never heard of the disease, but for the next year they would be able to think of little else. Kidneys afflicted with nephrosis expel proteins and blood cells along with waste matter. Fluids build up uncontrollably in the body tissue, causing grotesque edema and weight gain. As the disease progresses, blood cholesterol increases, antibody production dies off, and the massive accumulation of fluids can lead to peritonitis, blood poisoning, pneumonia, and death. The usual treatment was massive doses of steroids, which could have dangerous side effects—stunting of growth, obesity, glaucoma, and personality changes—but had managed to reduce the mortality rate of childhood nephrosis from 80 to 20 percent over the past twenty years.

They brought Allison to the Einstein Falk pediatric wing of Mount Sinai hospital for the first time in late March. I visited her there, as did my brother, comforting her as she was poked with needles and administered massive doses of prednisone for three weeks until fluids came pouring out of her body. But two weeks later, back at home, her body and face began to bloat again. It was awful to see the transformation: a once beautiful child now turned piggish, bloated, her arms and legs like balloons. Allison was conscious of how she looked, hated seeing her face in the mirror, hated being away from her dolls, her music, her friends, hated the clinical sterility of the Mount Sinai pediatric ward. This time she was treated with a powerful steroid known as triamcinolone, and again the symptoms abated.

By the fall Allison's disease was the sole focus of their lives. I would come back to the city on vacation to find my father and stepmother, often joined by my brother, obsessed with a daily ritual: testing the protein level of Allison's urine with a lab stick. A zero meant that Allison's kidneys were functioning normally, a three plus or a four plus meant they were expelling critical amounts of protein along with her urine. Her body would swell with fluids. Sometimes she gained ten pounds in ten days. Then, after a week or two, the steroids would take effect, she would expel the fluid in her urine, and the edema would subside. But she was also suffering now from the side effects of the daily doses of triamcinolone. She had high fevers. Her muscles became so weak that she could no longer stand. Drug-induced fat collected around her middle and her face. Other specialists, including the director of pediatrics and the children's kidney center at Albert Einstein Hospital in the Bronx, were brought in to examine her. He urged them to switch from triamcinolone back to predinisone. The prednisone didn't work: in December her weight ballooned from thirty to forty-seven pounds in two weeks.

In late January, I went for a week-long ski trip in Vermont. I left Princeton with a sense of foreboding. Things had not been going well for Allison in the weeks before I left. During the six days I skied at Killington, I considered phoning home to check on her condition. But I couldn't bring myself to do it—I couldn't face the bad news, if there was bad news. On Saturday morning I returned to Princeton and made the long-delayed call. Arlene's theatrical agent, a close friend, answered the phone. I knew at once that something was wrong. In a quavering voice she told me she would summon my father. He came to the phone moments later.

"Did something happen?" I asked. I already knew the answer.

That morning I rode the bus home to Manhattan, thinking of nothing but the scene that would meet me when I stepped through the threshold of their apartment. It played out just as I had imagined it would: my father and Arlene, shattered, sobbing, hugging each other and me in a long, desperate embrace in the doorway. Aunts and grandparents and cousins gathered in the living room. Tony had left the apartment, seeking solace from his friends at the High School of Performing Arts, just as he had sought comfort from them four months before when Marc died.

Nobody knew what had killed her. She had entered the hospital following another protein spillage. This time the doctors decided to treat her with cytoxan, a powerful form of chemo-therapy used on cancer patients. But one day into the treatment, she suddenly began to lose color, to become almost transparently white. Her hands and feet turned icy. Her veins began to shut down; it became almost impossible to draw blood. For the next twelve hours, as our father and Arlene paced the emergency room, Allison's doctors tried to stabilize her. Early on the morning of January 28, the pediatrician told them, stone-faced, that Allison had "expired."

It was a long, terrible day. Arlene remained in the bedroom, tranquilized, drifting in and out of consciousness. Relatives came and went. Even the elevator man was crying. I'd had my one good cry, and then I shut down. My cousins and I went out to see *Saturday Night Fever* in the afternoon, just to escape the oppressive atmosphere in the apartment.

Late that night, I sat alone in the living room, trying to take my mind off the day's events by watching *Saturday Night Live*. George Carlin was the guest host that night. Early into Carlin's monologue, my brother returned from a long evening out with his friends from Performing Arts. He sat across the room and watched me watching Carlin. I had the feeling he wanted to talk. I didn't know what to say. I was grieving, for Allison, for my father and Arlene, for the family, but I had long ago learned to bottle my emotions. I wanted my brother to be like me—strong exterior, tamped-down feelings.

"What?" I said. He must have detected the sharpness in my voice. He flinched. He mumbled something. I had my eye on the television. I laughed at something Carlin said. In Tony's eyes I sensed a silent reproach.

"What am I supposed to do about it?" I said. I was prac-tically shouting at him. "I can't change it. You can't change it. Nobody can change it." Tony said nothing. After another min-ute of silence, he stood up and disappeared into his bedroom. I sat there for another hour, staring at the TV screen, not really taking in a word.

It was not until years later, reading my brother's short story, that I gained a sense of how Allison's death had affected him:

> *He awoke to the ringing of a phone which shattered the morning stillness. He struggled out of bed, and lifted the receiver to his face.*
>
> > *"Hello?" he mumbled. He heard only emptiness.*
> >
> > *"Hello?" he mumbled again.*
> >
> > *"Rachel just died," the voice said on the other end.*
> >
> > *The voice faded out into a dial tone. He sank slowly down the wall to the floor. He tapped his head, then banged it continually against the wall behind him. . . . His eyes were shut, and several tears slipped out from under his eyelids, dripping down his cheeks. He lay prone for an hour, breathing deeply now and then, suffocating a cry at times. There was little else he could do. He found himself hovering over the small bed, in which the smiling bear and singing swan seemed asleep. He wished that he too, at this moment, could join them and forever sleep. But he knew that peace was impossible. He knelt before the bed and cried.*

In the months that followed, long after I returned to Princeton, others stepped in to fill the role that I had abdicated. By far the most important among them was my brother's closest friend from the High School of Performing Arts, Bob Barrett. Bob—a slight, curly-haired eighteen-year-old, a jazz aficionado and a devotee of Bertolt Brecht—had treated Allison like a little sister in those final months, visiting her in the hospital, presenting her with a single daisy each time he saw her, sitting on the floor beside her crib in her bedroom and entertaining her for hours. Two days after her death, our father remembered years later, Bob came through the front door holding a huge bouquet of daisies, and over the next few months he all but moved into the apartment, arriving with Tony from school on most afternoons or showing up to have supper with the family. He would sleep on the living room sofa, or on the day bed in my father's study, or on the floor behind a piece of furniture. It was as if, our father recalled, he was trying to offer himself as a partial substitute for what they had lost.

My brother took solace from Bob's constant presence. He had other good friends, but Bob was perhaps the only one in whom he could confide about Allison's death. Tony was insecure around some members of his Performing Arts clique—worried they perceived him as a clown, a nonentity—but from Bob he always felt unconditional love and acceptance.

Then, one evening in early October, Bob Barrett's father called the house. He and Bob had been jogging that morning in Central Park, he told our father, and had gone their separate ways with a plan to meet an hour later. Bob had not shown up, had not come home to change his clothes, had not appeared at his summer job. Did anyone there know where he was? Sorry, our father said, neither he nor Tony had seen him that day.

There was no word about Bob until the next morning. Bob's father phoned our father again. His voice sounded natural. They made small talk for a minute or two. Then my father asked if Bob had shown up.

"Yes," his father said. "I just identified his body at the morgue."

The morgue. The words did not sink in at first, our father remembered. Bob had been there two days earlier—healthy, vital, laughing. But Bob had suffered a freak asthma attack while running around the reservoir, and became asphyxiated before help could arrive. Our father reached my brother at the head-quarters for Carter Burden, the Democratic congressional candidate in Manhattan whose campaign he was helping to manage.

"I have terrible news," he said. "Bob's father just called."

"He's dead," Tony said.

"Yes."

"I knew it. Anybody who's close to me dies."

First Marc. Then Allison. Now Bob. The cruelty of fate seemed unrelenting, a sick joke. Sixty miles away in Princeton, I knew how alone my brother must be feeling. I wanted to console him—to make up for my coldness back in February. But it was all I could do to manage a one-minute call.

"Are you doing okay?" I asked.

"I'm fine."

"You're sure?"

"Yes, I'm fine."

"If you ever need to talk, you know you can give me a call."

"Thanks."

It was the only conversation we would ever have about Bob Barrett's death.

For many years afterward, whenever my father and I discussed my brother's embrace of faith, we always came back to those deaths. Tony would never confide to anyone—least of all me—how the loss of his two closest friends and sister in a single year had affected him. Yet I can easily imagine that the deaths must have heightened the sense of emptiness and meaninglessness in his life. He must have felt a desperate need for consolation.

My brother came to visit me at Princeton University just before my graduation in the late spring of 1979. I didn't really want him there; I didn't know what we would have to say to each other over an entire weekend. But I felt compelled to play the role of big brother. As the afternoon sun filtered through the sycamores and oaks and dappled the curving walkways of the campus, I gave him a tour, proudly showing off the stately Gothic dormitories, the gardens in full flower, and the ivy-cloaked mansions of Prospect Street. We tossed a Frisbee for a while, cooled off in the fountain of the Woodrow Wilson School plaza, then ate hamburgers and drank beer in the smoky cellar of The Annex tavern on Nassau Street. On Friday night we made the rounds of the end-of-year senior class parties on the verdant lawns of the lower campus. My brother seemed so wounded, so uncomfortable in his own skin, that I felt embarrassed by him. At one point I turned my back on him to join a group of friends in conversation, leaving him standing, awkwardly, alone. A friend rebuked me. How could I ignore my brother like that? she asked me. By Saturday afternoon, I felt like I had an albatross around my neck; I knew I wanted him to go home. I suggested he catch the six o'clock bus back to New York City.

"I can't stay through Sunday?"

"What for?" I said. "All the big parties were last night." I walked him to the bus stop on Nassau Street and practically pushed him onto the bus.

That September I embarked on a Princeton-in-Asia fellowship to teach English at a university in Tokyo for a year. Separated from my brother by twelve thousand miles, I brooded about my relationship with him. I was always brooding about my brother after the fact, it seemed, always regretting conversations that I hadn't had or time together that we hadn't spent. I began to correspond with him.

"Tokyo is crowded and ugly," I wrote in December. "The city is a jumble of faceless gray buildings, exposed wires, elevated train tracks. It is also a damned exciting city, filled with hopping entertainment districts and culture, and thousands of neon signs which light up explosively at night. All in all, it's not a bad place to live.... Are you still a Teddy Kennedy fanatic?" I asked. "I don't think he stands a chance against Jimmy Carter."

Tony wrote back a few weeks later. At Hobart College, he seemed to have gained his enthusiasm for life again. He was taking American politics and philosophy courses, and working a couple of hours a day for a New York state assemblyman. But the big news—the news that elated Arlene and my father and his friends from the High School of Performing Arts—was that he had found his way back to the theater.

The previous fall Tony had visited a friend who was starring in a campus production. Suddenly he realized how much he missed the stage, he wrote. He would enter the theater as the set was being constructed or rehearsal was in progress, and each time, he wrote, he had "a feeling of famine." My brother auditioned for a Hobart production of *Equus*, by the British playwright Peter Schaffer, the story of the tortured relationship between a psychiatrist, Martin Dysart, and Alan Strang, a seventeen-year-old stable hand who is committed to Dysart's mental hospital after blinding six horses in his care with a spike. Strang is a lost boy who finds meaning and transcendence in religion—not in the Christianity of his Bible-obsessed mother but in the worship of horses he deifies as Equus. My brother, who had been fascinated by the play since it ran on Broadway his freshman year at the High School of Performing Arts, auditioned for the part of Alan. Two days later, the director told him he had it.

"I felt joyous," he wrote me. But later, the doubts set in. He wondered whether he had the talent to bring such a complex character to life, and if he could withstand the scrutiny of five hundred pairs of eyes staring at his naked body on stage. Tony's uncertainty, however, began to fade as soon as he began rehearsals. "I worked harder on the play than I worked on anything in my life, including politics," he wrote.

My brother worked out for two months in the college gym in preparation for the play's climactic nude scene, in which Strang's sexual encounter with a female stable hand in front of his horse gods fills him with guilt—and leads to the horrific act of violence. Our father and Arlene saw the play on opening night and came back impressed. Tony's performance was movingly authentic, "staggering," they told me. After all the self-doubts at Performing Arts, the years of being overshadowed by more charismatic actors, Tony, they said, had come into his own—he had realized his talent. A friend from Peforming Arts remembered years later how Tony had been in high spirits during a trip down to Manhattan for a New Year's Eve party just after starring in *Equus*. He was excited about the play, the friend recalled, he was recommitted to acting, he had rediscovered his original joy in the theater.

Tony sent me a copy of the review in the college newspaper. "From his initial withdrawn and introspective entrance to the final emotional catharsis that climaxes the action," the critic wrote, "Tony Hammer's performance was as masterful a piece of acting as one could ask for." In his letter he evinced a sudden burst of self-confidence. Everyone was telling him how marvelously talented he was, how he must set aside his political ambitions and concentrate on acting. "So now, as you may be able to guess," he wrote me, "I want to spend my life creating in the theater."

We kept writing after I left Tokyo and began my solo backpacking trip across Southeast Asia. His college acting career was flourishing. In the spring of 1980 he starred in a production of the George Kaufman-Moss Hart 1930s comedy *The Man Who*

Came to Dinner. It was another triumph, but after the standing ovation and the three curtain calls, he felt depressed, he wrote to me: "A piece of me is absent; and my attention is drawn away from the page into some dark, distressing hole within. But I shall recover."

My brother was empowered by the characters he brought to life. His acting served partly as an escape, I now realize—an escape from self-doubt, from pain. But my brother's enthusiasm for Hobart seemed to last only as long as he was landing important roles onstage. After *The Man Who Came to Dinner*, the bubble seemed to burst. Tony was being considered for the leads in two plays—David Rabe's *Streamers* and *Henry IV, Part I*—but both productions were cancelled.

The fall of his junior year, he took a political philosophy course, and he became an ardent Marxist. Once again he seemed to be struggling to find a cause, something to believe in. The political arena obsessed him again; he wrote to friends, with his typical earnestness, that his life's mission was to try to change the world. Marx offered confirmation of something that he had always intuited: religion was a delusion. "As Marx pointed out," he wrote to his friends, "Man created God; not vice versa." Soon afterward, he boarded a plane for Tel Aviv.

ON A FRIGID FEBRUARY NIGHT SEVENTEEN years later, my brother and I, with Yankel and Ruchel asleep in the back of his station wagon, sped north through the Catskill Mountains along the New York State Thruway. The four-lane ribbon of tarmac wound through pine forests and rolling hills toward Albany and Lake Placid and the Canadian border. From the cassette deck, a Jewish children's chorus sang martial hymns about the glory of being a soldier for God.

"WE'RE IN THE ARMY YES THAT'S RIGHT.
WE FIGHT FOR THE TORAH WITH ALL OUR MIGHT.
HASHEM GAVE US THE TORAH, WHICH TOLD US WHAT TO DO.
AND I'M SO PROUD THAT I'M A JEW."

A light dusting of snow sprinkled the woods and fields of the Catskills, gradually thickening to a solid white blanket as we ventured farther north. Warm air blasted from the heater in my brother's ancient car, a gift from our mother a decade earlier. I reached behind the seat into a bag filled with snacks and pulled out a strawberry roll. "Say a *barucha*," my brother said. He was like a Jewish drill sergeant, tirelessly reminding me to perform the mitzvahs.

We had been on the road for three hours, heading for Tosh, a highly devout Hasidic community on a windswept prairie north of Montreal. My brother had become a frequent visitor since he began his progression from Americanized ultra-Orthodoxy to Hasidism. It was a place that was coming to play an increasingly important role in his life, and he had invited me to join him on this wintertime pilgrimage. The Tosh rebbe was one of the great tsaddikim of the Jewish world, and the two thousand Hasidic inhabitants of Tosh lived as close to God, my brother declared, as was possible on earth. Although his relationship with the Lev Tohor Rov had come to an abrupt end three months earlier, my brother was still enamored of the mystical Hasidic style of worship. The Tosh rebbe represented the more acceptable, conventional face of Hasidism: he was a Holocaust survivor who came from a centuries-old dynasty in Hungary. Even Ahuva had made a few journeys to Tosh over the last five years, and she expressed no qualms about her husband's deepening relationship with the rebbe.

I felt a surprising degree of ease with my brother as we sat together in the warm coccoon of the station wagon. It was the third weekend that I had spent with him since my initial November visit, and we were growing steadily more comfortable and spontaneous around each other. I had even consented to calling him Tuvia; it was impossible to think of my brother as Tony anymore. He had, I realized, shed himself of that secular identity forever, and there seemed to be no point in denying the truth. The car ride invigorated me. I had never taken a lengthy road trip with my brother before, and I was determined to take advantage of our time together. There was so much, I realized, that I had never asked him.

•   •   •

"Tell me about your wedding," I said as we rolled on through the darkness. "Was Ahuva the first woman they introduced you to?"

I had worried that the wedding might be too private a subject for him to discuss, but he showed no hesitation. "The second," he said. "Sheindi Rosenman set it up. The first moment that I saw Ahuva coming up the steps of the house I knew she was the right one. And she said the same thing about me. We spent an hour talking the first night, we talked another four hours, then another five hours, and then it was pretty much sealed."

"Three meetings, and then you were engaged?"

"Well, it wasn't that easy. Ahuva's boss and her rabbi objected. They had seen me davening in synagogue and they thought I was, well, wild."

"Wild?"

"Too emotional. Too carried away with the love of Hashem. I was always like that. But they said it was inappropriate. They got the shidduch called off."

I was not surprised to discover that even during his early days as a Litvisher Jew, my brother had hovered on the more extreme fringes of religious devotion.

"How did that make you feel?" I asked.

"Devastated. But that night I had this dream. Grandma Bea appeared, and she said, 'Give her a call, tell her you love her, that's the best thing you should do.' "

"Did you call her?"

"I almost didn't have the courage," he admitted. "But I did call her up one night. Ahuva told me later she was shocked. For a boy to call a girl out of the blue, when the shidduch was called off? It wasn't heard of. It was beyond the bounds of modesty. But two days later, Rabbi Rosenman learned that all the objections from the two sides had been removed. I think the phone call opened up a door to heaven and made these men relent. The next day I got engaged. I went to a lake and asked her to marry me. Then we went back to Monsey and we made a *l'chaim*."

We passed the exit for Saranac Lake, where my brother and I had gone to summer camp the year after our parents' divorce. I had been fourteen, he was ten. I asked him if he remembered the day that our father had come into my bedroom and told us he was moving out. He nodded.

"You cried and I did nothing," he said.

"Were you expecting it?" I asked.

My brother shrugged. "I think that was my reaction to everything. I was placid. You were very clear, creative, and I was just following along."

"That's the way you felt?"

"That's the way it was."

"I was traumatized," I told him.

"I remember."

"I didn't want to admit to anyone that our parents had gotten divorced. I had friends over for the night once after the divorce, and I told them, 'My dad is sleeping in the bedroom over there, so be quiet.' The next morning, they said, 'Your father was in there?' I said, 'He left before you woke up. You didn't hear him?' "

"It was devastating," my brother said.

"It was an awful time."

We pulled off the thruway to an illuminated service area. Nestled in the rear compartment, the children did not stir. My brother smeared a bagel with a dab of lox spread, said the barucha, ate the sandwich quickly, and then steered the car back onto the thruway.

"You want to know why Dad suffered?" he asked me suddenly. "Because he wrote for the wrong magazines."

I rolled my eyes. Hurt by the way he had been rejected by our father, my brother seemed to make a hobby of disparaging him. He interpreted his prolonged financial troubles as further evidence of the betrayals of the secular world, and of God's punishment of those who turn their back on Him.

"What magazines?" I said. "You mean *Playboy* and *Penthouse*?"

He flinched. "Don't say the words—I don't want the words in the air."

"Sorry."

"He sold himself out for gelt. What he should do now is move to a little house in Massachusetts, for three hundred dollars a month, and wait until it's time to surrender his nashama to Hashem."

"That's ridiculous," I said, amused.

"Why should he live in New York City? What's he going to do? Wait for them to decide the Luciano book is credible? Dad had all the *kaylem*—the tools—to become a great tsaddik, if only he'd gone to a yeshiva. He had a great heart, a great analytical mind, a great memory. He could sit and study for hours. But he didn't have the right upbringing."

Later we began to talk about my brother's college days. "I always wished that I'd seen you on stage in *Equus* in 1979," I said.

He turned away. "I don't want to talk about that. That was a terrible sin. I had to do *tshuva* for that."

"*Tshuva*? What was so sinful about a great performance?"

"It was one of the three cardinal sins—killing somebody, immorality, and idol worship."

"What, taking off your clothes?"

"Not the nudity—the role itself. Worshiping the horse."

"But you were acting a part."

"It doesn't make a difference. Bringing such concepts into the world is one of the worst things that a Jew can do. The whole reason for a Jew to exist is to declare to the world, 'There is only one God.' If a person says, 'Jump in the fire or say that there is another God besides Him,' a person is obligated to jump into the fire."

Shortly after two o'clock in the morning, exhausted, we arrived at the floodlit plaza marking the Canadian border. My brother stiffened as we approached the booth. Some of his Hasidic friends had been stopped and searched by American immigration officials while on their way to Tosh, forced to wait for an hour or more while their cars and luggage were pulled apart. Such petty harassment was, my brother said, another reminder that the Jews were still in the *galus*—the exile—never truly welcome anywhere they dwelled, looking forward to the day when Moshiach, the Messiah, a descendant of King David, appeared on earth to lead them to Zion.

The triumphant arrival of the Messiah, he said, would be foreshadowed by the rise and fall of a terrible tyrant like Hitler. It would be the most catastrophic upheaval in human history. A sorting out of humanity would follow. Jews who had faithfully kept God's mitzvahs would stream back to Israel, to live again in the state of *kadusha*, holiness, that existed at the time of the First Temple. The Jews—religious Jews—would ascend to the top of the new world order. The gentiles would seek out the Messiah as well, and happily labor in the fields of their Jewish masters for the rest of their days. And a Third Temple, built from the prayers of all the Jews who ever lived in exile, would rise in Jerusalem.

"When is all of this supposed to happen?" I asked.

"It should be by the year 6000, according to the predictions—two hundred twenty years from now. But it could even take place in our lifetime. It could happen tomorrow. There are rebbes who sleep every night with their satchels packed, waiting for the Messiah to arrive."

The arrival of the Messiah was subject to delays, he said. The failure of the Jews to do tshuva—to repent for their transgressions—could prolong the galus indefinitely. And there was also the matter of the gentiles. "Any time a goy does a Yid a favor," my brother said, "another hour is added to the galus."

"So you're saying that gentiles shouldn't do Jews any favors?"

"The point is that they have to be paid back immediately. Otherwise it all goes into the account book. No good deed ever goes unanswered by God."

"The gentiles want the galus to continue?"

"Of course. They're on top. They're riding high. The Jews are the bottom. It's going to be reversed when the exile ends."

"How can you say that the Jews are on the bottom?"

"I'm not talking about the Israeli state. I'm not talking about Steven Spielberg. I'm talking about the frum Jews. The real Jews."

Above downtown Montreal, two tanned bodies caressed each other on a huge illuminated billboard beneath the words: CUBA LE SOLEIL. My brother flinched—as he always did from any suggestion of sex. He had turned into a stern, unbending moralist. Sexual relations between a husband and wife were holy, he maintained, as long as one never took one's mind off God during the act and reminded oneself that he was fulfilling the mitzvah of producing children. But he considered any other type of sex an *aveireh*—a transgression. The hymen, he informed me, was created by God to provide proof of a woman's virtuousness before her marriage. "Is there any firmer evidence than that of Hashem's existence?" he asked me.

In Boisbriand, fifteen miles northeast of Montreal, we passed a General Motors plant, a hulking complex surrounded by empty fields. Just beyond the factory we saw the sign for Tosh, then turned left down an ice-crusted street lined on both sides with eight-foot snow drifts. Yellow globes cast an eerie light on the bungalows and low-slung apartments that lined the avenue. A heavily wrapped figure in black hustled up the steps of a red-brick yeshiva, books nestled under his arm.

"It's four in the morning," I said, staring.

My brother nodded. "It's a great mitzvah to study on the day before Shabbos," he said, pulling into the ice-covered drive-way of the large wood-shingle house where we would be spending the night.

My brother's paradise on earth, I discovered the next morning, was an austere enclave almost completely cut off from the out-side world. A howling Arctic wind blew snow across rue Beth Halevy, the settlement's U-shaped main street. Blandly func-tional red and yellow-brick apartment blocks lined the avenue. Beyond the settlement, snow-covered tundra stretched toward distant clumps of fir trees, enhancing the sense of isolation. Bundled-up, black-clad figures shuffled across an undulating crust of ice that would likely remain on the ground until late March. I saw no women: they were indoors, my brother said approvingly, tending to their children and cooking Shabbos dinner. There was not much gender mixing in Tosh, nor was there much to do besides pray, study, and wait for an audience with the Tosh rebbe—who had, it was said, cured cancer and made some ac-olytes wealthy with his shrewd investment advice.

Ferenz Lowy, the Tosh rebbe, epitomized a life lived in

absolute devotion to the Almighty. One of the last links to a golden age of Hasidism that had ended with the Holocaust, Lowy was renowned as both a Talmudic scholar and a holy man. When the Germans marched into Hungary in 1944, Lowy's sect was annihilated, along with most other Hasidic communities, and a great oral tradition and body of Jewish literature destroyed with it. Lowy was dispatched to Auschwitz, where he spent his days davening in the barracks, dismissed as meshugge—crazy—by his Jewish supervisor.

After the war Lowy settled in Austria with a few survivors, then received a vision from God telling him to rebuild his movement in Quebec. So in 1951 Lowy and eighteen families arrived in Montreal—the first Hasidim ever to set foot in Canada. Eleven years later, they abandoned the big city, claiming that it was too materialistic and corrupt, and purchased 106 hectares of farmland in the Catholic outpost of Boisbriand, fifteen miles north of Montreal. Tosh had since grown to three hundred families—more than two thousand Hasidim. Another six thousand disciples were scattered in small communities around the world—in New York, London, Belgium, and Israel. Hundreds of other Jews, such as my brother, also trooped into the remote community on Shabbos and during *yom tovs*, often waiting for days for a two-minute audience with the tsaddik.

The Tosh Hasidim spoke Yiddish as their first—and sometimes only—language. All wore the costume of their ancestors in the shtetl, including the long, dangling side curls, the ankle-length black overcoat, or rekel, and, on Sabbaths and holidays, the ceremonial beaver fur *streimel*. Most had as little to do with the secular world as possible. Only by sealing themselves off from Western influence, they felt, had they been able to maintain the purity of their religion and to keep their community intact.

"Where does the Tosh rebbe rank among the leaders of the Jews?" I asked my brother as we shuffled over the ice toward the synagogue for evening services. My brother had lent me a white scarf that I had wrapped a half dozen times around my face to protect myself from the relentless wind, but the bitter gusts sliced through the thin wool like a knife through butter. I sank lower into the hoodless parka, cursing to myself with each stinging blast of frigid air, trying to remember the last time I had felt so cold.

"He's a tsaddik, but the rebbe doesn't come to the ankles of people two generations before him," my brother acknowledged, his voice muffled by the wool scarf. "Each generation is further away from hearing the voice of Hashem on Mount Sinai. People today look at their rebbe, and compared to their rebbe's rebbe, he's a yeshiva boy."

"So who do you consider to be the greatest tsaddik?"

"The Rugachuver Goan, for instance, never got a haircut, because it required taking off his yarmulke, which would have required him to stop learning. He read all day standing up so he wouldn't fall asleep. The *rebbetzin*—the rabbi's wife—put pillows around him so he didn't hurt himself." My brother—who once idolized people such as Al Pacino and Teddy Kennedy—had developed some odd new role models, I thought.

The Tosh synagogue was as formal and stately as my brother's neighborhood shul, Bais Iyel, was informal and modest. Its vaulted ceilings soared fifty feet above a shimmering white tile floor. A white satin curtain shielded the Holy Ark of the Torah. Elegant brass chandeliers dangled from the ceiling. Yet there was an austerity about this house of worship. The only representative imagery was a mural behind the Holy Ark that depicted, in pastel shades , the classical facade of King Solomon's Temple. Above the Temple shimmered three golden crowns, representing the three branches of Judaism: kings, the descendants of David; priests, the descendants of Aharon; and the Torah scholars. My brother and I took seats in the balcony, high above a sea of five hundred Hasidic worshipers, and watched as, far below us, the Tosh rebbe—a stooped figure draped in a white gown—read from the Torah in a feeble voice, his gnarled white fingers dancing across the yellow parchment.

"We're eating by Rabbi Krausz tonight," my brother said as we stepped back into the frigid night. The Hasidic influence now permeated his speech. People didn't study or eat or play "at" somebody's house, they ate "by" him—a transliteration of the Yiddish word *bei*, meaning "at." Instead of asking, "How are you doing?" my brother always said, "Where are you holding?" That was a literal translation of the Yiddish expression *Wie hauft die?* It implied: what section of the Talmud are you currently reading? His conversations were sprinkled with Yiddish words. The goal of a mensch, he said, was to bring his nashama, or soul, near the Abeshter, or God. A Jew must bring out his *koichois*, or inner strength, to conquer his *yetzer hara*, or evil inclination, and strive for *kadisha*, holiness. My brother took his leave of people by saying either "*Zeit gesundt*"—you should be healthy—or "*Yasher koach*"—you should go forward with strength, the words that God spoke to Moshe Rebbenu after Moshe smashed the tablets. "If a Yid wants to bring his nashama close to the Abeshter, he has to hold by the mitzvahs," my brother once told me excitedly. Talking to him often left me dizzy.

My brother and I knocked on the door of a ground-floor apartment just down Beth Halevy Street from the shul. It was opened by a huge Hasid whose face was almost obscured by a leonine black beard. "Good Shabbos, Good Shabbos," he exclaimed. A welcome blast of warm air from the apartment's electric heating system wafted over me. He grabbed my hand in a meaty paw and led my brother and me into his cramped dining room, sparsely decorated with the usual portraits of white-bearded tsaddikim and a case filled with silver candelabra and kiddush cups.

"So you work for *Newsweek?*" he asked. "You were the one who broke the Monica story?"

"No, that wasn't me," I said, surprised. "But how did you know?"

"Believe me, I know."

Rabbi Shlomo Krausz was one of Tosh's more worldly residents, a real estate broker who commuted to Montreal on weekdays and played regular host to pilgrims from around the world on the Sabbath. A glance around the table showed an intriguing sartorial diversity. Across from me sat a pair of young Hasidim from Israel, clad in the traditional eighteenth-century shtetl dress. Beside them, and a striking contrast, perched a Sephardic Jew from Morocco. A slight, dark man with a gray-streaked goatee, he peered out from under a peculiar, almost Napoleonic sable hat. Instead of the usual black coat, he wore a sharp business suit. Later I learned that he practiced law in northern Quebec. Krausz's small sons were everywhere, wearing identically braided peyyes, black-and-white-checked vests, and black fedoras. Descending in size, they looked like a set of Hasidic nesting dolls.

"I've got seven boys, four girls," Krausz said proudly, throwing his arms around the sunken shoulders of two of his sons. "The Torah says that if you have seven boys, you're guaranteed a spot in the Garden of Eden."

Krausz's sons kept running to the kitchen and returning with heaped plates of food. Where were the women? I asked my brother. Embarrassed, he explained that Krausz's four daughters and his wife were not only forbidden to sit at the same table with the men, they were obliged to keep out of sight. I spotted them clustered in the kitchen when I got up to use the bathroom. All wore frumpy flowered print dresses with puffy sleeves, sewn from the same rough cotton fabric. They were eating around the sink, standing up.

"So they're forced to spend all of Shabbos in the kitchen?" I asked, incredulous.

My brother shrugged. "They look at it as if the men are forced to be out here."

Women in Tosh lived a confined existence, he told me. They were forbidden to drive or to work, and discouraged from having contact with men other than their husbands. They shaved their heads and wore head scarves. My brother thought this was all a good idea. Wigs, he explained, were too seductive, arousing lustful thoughts and distracting men from their obligations to God. He had often asked Ahuva to rid herself of her *sheitels* and adopt the Hasidic look, but she had refused. I was not surprised to learn that Ahuva had also rejected my brother's repeated entreaties to move to the village.

Midway through the meal, the discussion turned to the Tosh rebbe. "What makes this rebbe so special?" I asked the other guests. "Why come all the way from Israel to see him?"

"It's not the kind of thing you can explain," said one of the Israelis dismissively. Rabbi Krausz poured himself his second tall glass of Kahlua and Coke. "Let somebody try," he said.

The Moroccan began to speak, but it was difficult to understand him. He wore dentures, and they seemed to fit poorly in his mouth. He sprayed food particles across the table as he launched into his story.

Krausz glared at him. "Finish chewing your food," he ordered.

"Wha?" asked the Moroccan, spitting more flecks. "Wha did you say?"

"Swallow your food before you speak," Krausz said.

The Moroccan paused, sipped some wine, then tried again. "I knew a civil engineer in Montreal, an observant Jew," he began. My brother leaned forward on his elbows, listening intently. "One day the Canadian government asked him to help build a dam in Upper Volta, deep in the Sahara Desert. Well, this Jew was eager for the work, but he wondered how he would keep kosher and celebrate the High Holy Days so far from home. The government assured him it would deliver him kosher food once a week, and fly him back to Canada three times a year.

"So the engineer went to see the Tosh rebbe. He didn't speak Yiddish, so he asked me to translate," said the Moroccan. "He said, 'Rebbe, should I take the job?' The rebbe's head drooped. He sat with his chin on his chest. Five minutes went by. We thought, is he asleep? Suddenly, the rebbe raised his head and screamed, '*Nein! Nein!*' The engineer pleaded with him. 'What can I do?' he said. 'I need to make a living. I have a family to support.' Again, the Tosh rebbe said, '*Nein!* We'll give you a job here in the community.' This man was not the type to disobey the words of a tsaddik. He told the government he couldn't accept the job. He went to work instead as a bookkeeper in Tosh."

The Moroccan sipped his wine. "Three months later the engineer came up to me in shul. He looked pale, in shock. 'How did the rebbe know?' he asked. 'Know what?' I said. A coup had taken place in Upper Volta. The army had seized power, killed the president, called off the dam project, and jailed and tortured the entire team of engineers as spies."

The next morning after prayers, the Tosh rebbe's private secretary shouted to me and my brother across the crowded synagogue: "Come to a *tish* at the rebbe's house." Every Saturday afternoon, my brother explained, the rebbe hosted a communal Sabbath meal known as a tish for guests in the community. The tish was one of the customs that distinguished Hasidism from all other sects of Judaism, he said, and a rite that I had to experience.

The tish—Yiddish for table—took place in the Tosh

rebbe's dining room, a high-ceilinged hall painted baby blue. In the center of the room stood a long table draped in white linen, surrounded by three tiers of wooden benches. A turbulent sea of men wearing black robes, streimels, beards, and peyyes—some thick as ropes, others coiled tightly like telephone cords—spilled over the benches. The room smelled of gefilte fish and unwashed bodies. My brother and I squeezed into the first row behind and above the table. I was the only one of the guests not wearing black, but nobody appeared to notice.

At the head of the table, in a high-back carved oak chair upholstered with red leather, the Tosh rebbe surveyed his guests. He reminded me of children's book portraits of Merlin the magician. Silky peyyes flowed down his parchment-like cheeks, a massive streimel dwarfed his head, and a flowing snow white beard spilled down his white linen gown. He began to slice the air feebly with karate-chop waves of his right hand, turning toward each member of his flock standing before him. The Hasidim leaned from the benches and chopped back feverishly, eager to catch the rebbe's glance and receive his blessing.

A clean-shaven yeshiva boy approached the rebbe from behind, bearing a golden goblet filled with wine. The rebbe accepted the chalice with trembling white hands, mumbled an inaudible blessing, and sipped. All around me Hasidim began to chant with joy. The sound rolled over me like the blast from a great church organ:

Ay yay yay yay yay
Ay yay yay yay yay

My brother clasped my hand and began to sing. Then the young Hasid to my right grabbed my other hand. We began to sway back and forth. At first I was silent, but as the chanting welled up around me, I began to lose my inhibitions. It was impossible not to feel stirred by so much emotion. I gripped the damp hands of my brother and the stranger on my right, and joined in singing the wordless melody. Several Hasidim grinned at me across the table. Their smiles emboldened me, and I started to chant even louder.

As we sang and rocked back and forth, the meal proceeded. Yeshiva boys brought the rebbe two giant challahs—bulbous loaves as big as medicine balls. The rebbe's assistant sliced him a piece of bread with a pearl-handled knife, and the rebbe uttered another blessing. The assistant began to toss bits of challah down the table and pass the bread into the benches above and behind us. Soon plates laden with cornbread and minced herring came sailing toward us on a sea of black.

"Watch him. He never takes too much," my brother said, pointing at the rebbe. "He brings the fork up to his mouth, he doesn't go down to the food. He's showing his control over his earthly appetites."

The tish, my brother explained, was a holy act with multiple layers of meaning. It engraved in a person "tremendous love for other Jews." It was a symbolic reenactment of the ritual sacrifices that had taken place at the Temple in Jerusalem—and it brought the Tosh rebbe and his acolytes into a sacred bond.

Suddenly, the man to my right grabbed my hand in a vise-like grip and pulled me from the table. Scores of Hasidim surged from the benches toward the front of the room. The meal was ending, and the Hasidim were rushing to receive a morsel of food directly from the Tosh rebbe's hand. The sweaty knot of humanity shoved and elbowed one another in their efforts to be first in line.

"These guys are pushy," I yelled to my brother, who was separated from me by a half dozen exuberant young Hasidim.

"They're pushing with love," my brother replied.

I was compressed inside a scrum. Excited cries in Yiddish

wafted over me. An elbow caught my ribs, a knee dug into my lower back. As I neared the table, the black sea parted, and a dozen hands shoved and tugged me forward. The rebbe's assistant, standing protectively beside his leader, motioned for me to approach. The rebbe gazed impassively from his high-back chair, surrounded by stern-looking, bearded minions. I extended my hand. With quivering fingers the ancient patriarch scooped a rectangular lump of black potato kugel from a silver platter and placed it directly onto my palm. The sticky mass scorched my hand through the paper napkin. *"Danke,"* I said. He nodded, expressionless, and I was swept aside to make way for the next in line.

ALTHOUGH MY BROTHER AND I WERE GROW-ing more comfortable with each other's company, my visits to Monsey still required constant vigilance. I must never, he warned me repeatedly, bring up the Lev Tohor Rov in front of the family. I was also to say nothing to the children about the divorce of our parents, our father's remarriage, or anything else that would "confuse" them about what constituted acceptable Jewish conduct. I was careful never to allude to my slippage from the Jewish faith, the fact that I never went to synagogue in Los Angeles, never observed the Sabbath, and had doubts about the existence of God. Most difficult of all was the concealment of a part of my life which I could never share with my brother. I knew that my mother had told him about my girlfriend, a non-Jew from England whom I had met in Africa four years earlier. But I also knew that he considered a relationship with a gentile one of the worst sins a Jew could commit. He had never forgiven our father for marrying Arlene. After my first Sabbath visit to Monsey, Arlene received a letter from my brother. It politely thanked her for being a surrogate mother to him during his adolescence and expressed regret for his many years of cool silence toward her. None of this, however, affected his position toward our father. The Torah was clear: Jews who married non-Jews violated the Almighty's laws and could never be forgiven.

My brother appeared to have compartmentalized what knowledge he had of my relationship. I never brought up the subject—it seemed too inflammatory. We maintained a strange fiction that I lived alone in Los Angeles with my two dogs, and that while I was visiting my brother's family in Monsey "a friend" was taking care of them. If I was to have any relationship with my brother at all, I realized, it would have to be on his terms. To some extent, this meant living a lie.

But it was not easy to keep myself constantly in check. One early spring afternoon, the day before the eight-day festival of Passover, I took a long walk through Monsey's quiet streets with my nephews Yankel and Yosef Dov. The first buds were appearing on the maple trees along Carlton Road, and a couple of ultra-Orthodox boys were playing catch with a softball in front of their homes. I was curious to find out just how much exposure my brother's sons had to such secular diversions.

"Who's your favorite Yankee, Yankel?" I asked.

"Bernie Williams," he replied without hesitation.

"Do you watch the Yankees on TV?"

He shook his head. "No. But a friend has a computer baseball game at home that I sometimes play."

"Your father doesn't mind that you're playing baseball on a computer?"

"He says it's okay on a computer, but not on TV."

"Have you ever watched television?"

"For a few minutes, sometimes, at the mall."

As we turned into Blauvelt Road, Yankel's next statement caught me off guard.

"You know what happens to a goy when he dies?" he said.

"What?"

"First the worms eat him up, and then he gets burned by fire."

"Fire?" I repeated weakly, stunned.

"They don't even know who to daven to, the goyim, they daven to idols."

My patience snapped. "I don't think I buy any of this stuff."

Both boys looked at me, then at each other. "What?" asked Yankel.

"I'm not sure I believe in God," I said.

They stared at me, then edged away as if I were contaminated. Moments later, my brother called me from the living room. "Yehoshua?"

He must have overheard me.

"Shut the door," he said, staring sternly from an armchair. I obeyed, feeling like a small child summoned to the principal's office.

There was a long silence. He closed the Talmud volume he had been reading and regarded me fixedly. "My children are like rubies to me," he said. "They're the most precious objects in my life."

"I understand," I muttered.

"The foundations of a child's belief are weak. If they start hearing doubts, those foundations might collapse."

"I'm sorry." My voice was almost a whisper.

"I will not have those beliefs questioned, do you understand? If I hear that kind of talk again, I'll have to reconsider allowing you into our house."

"Understood," I said.

I was filled with remorse. But later that afternoon, as I lay in my basement bedroom, that remorse started to congeal into anger and resentment. My brother had deliberately created an information vacuum around his children, depriving them of the ability to make their own choices. In my brother's view he was merely shielding them from corrupting influences. But the effort to control their thinking seemed unreasonably harsh to me— and counterproductive. Forbidden and seductive ideas would no doubt seep into their world, and I wondered whether my brother's approach would ultimately backfire.

For weeks I had been intrigued by the prospect of spending Passover, or Pesach, in my brother's home. It was the one Jewish holiday that our family had observed each year when we were growing up, the strongest reminder of our Jewish roots. Every April my parents, brother, and I would pile into our 1966 Chrysler sedan and drive two hours on the Merritt Parkway to our paternal grandparents' home in West Hartford. A crowd of relatives was always on hand, including our great-grandmother Lena, a sparrow-like woman from the Ukrainian town of Vinnitsa who had emigrated to the United States in 1902. She would peck my brother and me on the cheek and greet us in a thick Yiddish accent, calling us *bubbeleh*. Then, at the head of the table, Grandpa Moe, an imposing man with a bald head and ever present cigarette, would rush through an English edition of the Haggadah. He would sprinkle irreverent comments about Moses and the exodus of the Jews into the service, which was over and done with in thirty minutes.

Pesach in my brother's home was transformed into an event almost unrecognizable from the watered-down seders of our youth. The exodus from Egypt was clearly a living event to my brother. The deliverance from bondage and the miracles in the Sinai Desert confirmed to him the heroic destiny of the Jewish people. As sundown approached, the entire family threw itself frantically into a last-minute sweep for *chamitz*—bread crumbs, crackers, any one of five types of grain that has come into contact with water for eighteen minutes or longer. The Torah commands Jews to remove chamitz from their homes to commemorate the hasty flight of the Israelites from Egypt, when they baked unleavened bread, or matzoh. My brother took off his shiny black gown, or *bekesher*, and rolled up his sleeves. With a lit candle in one hand and a feather and wooden spoon in the other, he dove behind a black leather couch and emerged triumphantly a moment later, carrying the petrified remains of a long-lost croissant.

"Chamitz," he declared, handing the offending object to Yankel, who brought it to a backyard pit to be ritually burned the following day.

Just before sundown, my brother donned a white *kittel*, or ceremonial gown, that he had first put on at his wedding and subsequently wore only during Yom Kippur and Pesach. He propped up pillows on the couch, where he would recline throughout the meal, he said, "to remind us of the Jews' flight from Egypt and our new status as free men—as kings." Then he sat at the head of the table, clutching his Haggadah, ready for his starring role in the evening's drama. "You're going to see your brother's Performing Arts training now," Ahuva told me. "He lives for this moment on the stage."

The seder lasted seven hours. The procession of Passover rituals followed a slow and stately course. I sat at my brother's side, trying to remain alert as he read through the entire Haggadah, telling the story of the exodus from Egypt, a tradition known in Hebrew as V'higadetah L'bincha, or "You must tell your sons." It was midnight before the first course appeared on the table. By three o'clock in the morning, most of the children were curled in their chairs, fast asleep. My eyes were glazing over—but Tuvia was still singing energetically from the Haggadah.

. . .

My brother's busy social schedule during Passover reminded me again of one of the central attractions of the ultra-Orthodox world: its powerful feeling of community. My brother seemed to have built himself a surrogate family here in Monsey, a circle as tight-knit as his clique at the High School of Performing Arts. But the wildness and irreverence of his high school crowd could not have been more different from the rigidity and reverence of this circle.

The morning after the seder, my brother invited me to a party held by Rabbi Chaim Wolf Weiss, an old friend who had presided over his wedding fourteen years earlier. Rabbi Weiss, his wife, Raizel, and their nine children lived a few blocks away, in the heart of Kaser, a village of Viznitz Hasidim. Kaser was a cluster of twenty-five streets and alleys built around a soaring white-brick synagogue with a twin-towered Romanesque facade—a near replica of the Viznitz sect's original synagogue in the Carpathian Mountains of Rumania. A wealthy Viznitz Hasid who had amassed a fortune investing in Rockland County real estate had donated $3 million for construction of the shul in 1993, and the building was taken as a sign of both the growing prosperity and the rapid cultural renaissance of the Hasidim in America.

But while a private fortune had paid for the Viznitz Synagogue, most of the seven hundred and fifty families in the village lived in poverty. Perhaps two-thirds of the Viznitz Hasidim were dependent on public assistance—welfare payments, food stamps, and subsidized housing. The vast majority scraped by as yeshiva instructors, bus drivers, clerks in kosher supermarkets, and other low-paying jobs. Rabbi Weiss was an electrician, although he had retired from his trade so he could intensify his study of the Talmud, and now subsisted—as Tuvia did—on a small monthly stipend paid to him by the kollel.

Flanked by my brother's two oldest sons, I crossed the temple square. Children played amid the wood-frame skeletons of a construction site—a sign of Kaser's rapid expansion. The village, I had learned, had one of the highest birth rates in the world: an average of eight children per family. A few children circled around the streets on bright red scooters—a vehicle I had not encountered since my own childhood. Grand Rabbi Mordechai Hager, the Viznitz rebbe, had banned bicycles from the village because they were supposedly too dangerous. "Whenever we see a kid going by on a scooter," Yankel told me, "we know it's a Viznitz kid."

Chaim Wolf Weiss's small apartment was filled with members of Weiss's large clan and several friends and neighbors. Yosef, Yankel, and I arrived ahead of the rest of our family. The apartment's tidiness was in marked contrast to the disorder of my brother's home. Seated in a rocking chair, a white-bearded patriarch—Weiss's father-in-law—studied me.

"You're Tuvia's brother?" Weiss's father-in-law asked, looking surprised. My brother had embraced his faith so wholeheartedly that it was widely assumed, I had learned, that he had been born into an observant home. He was, as Ahuva would say, "as frum as they come."

With a nosiness that took me aback, the old man inquired how my brother was supporting his family. As far as I knew, he hadn't worked since Ahuva forced him to quit his job at the Lev Tohor Rov's yeshiva. I told the old man that as far as I knew, the only occupation my brother had was voluntary work with the local burial society. The Chevra Kadisha was a squadron of ultra-Orthodox men who bathed and shrouded newly deceased members of the community according to Talmudic rules. Sometimes my brother would accompany the body to the cemetery and supervise the burial service. On those occasions, he always made sure to keep his tsitsis tucked inside his pants, he told me, so as not to offend the dead by reminding them that they could no longer perform the 613 mitzvahs.

The old man waved his hand. "The Chevra Kadisha doesn't pay. What does he do to make money? Does he just study the whole day?"

He seemed more preoccupied with financial responsibilities than other Hasidim I had met.

The children looked embarrassed. "My mother runs a kindergarten," Yankel offered.

"Morah Hammer's Happy Home," Weiss's daughter chimed in.

"What?" asked the old man, who was hard of hearing. "She works for Pataki?"

"Happy. Happy Home," the daughter yelled in her grandfather's ear.

"What do you do?" he asked me.

"I'm a writer," I said.

"You're writing a book about the Jews?"

I hesitated. "Kind of," I said.

"Kind of?" he snapped. "What do you mean, kind of?"

"I'm writing about baal tshuvas," I stammered. "I'm trying to understand why so many assimilated Jews are returning to their religious roots."

"You want to know why?" he said. "Look at what's happening in this culture. Society is going down. People are shooting each other dead in high schools. And it's not just America. I just got back from Israel. In Israel even the policemen, the sanitation men, they're becoming baal tshuvas."

A tall, handsome Hasid with opaque dark eyes and an aquiline nose joined in the conversation. Why, he asked me, did everyone attack the Hasidim for having so many children? "I had a friend who was in an airport in Australia," the Hasid told me. "He was with the whole family, waiting to get on his flight. This German came up to him, looked at all the kids, and asked,

'When are you going to stop?' My friend replied, 'When I reach six million.' "

Men sat at one table, women at another. The arrangement was a little looser than at Tosh, but mixing among the sexes was still discouraged in Weiss's home. The slim, fidgety man next to me wore the fedora, dark suit, and tie of the Litvisher Jews. He looked exactly the way my brother had before he fell in with the Lev Tohor Rov. I sized him up instantly as a baal tshuva. He introduced himself as Moshe Hertzberg—formerly Mark—and looked back and forth across the table between me and my brother.

"I'm trying to see the resemblance between you and Tuvia," he said.

"Take away his beard and you'll see it," I replied.

"I'd rather not take away his beard."

Raizel Weiss, plain and plump, leaned across the women's table. "You look like your nieces and nephews," she told me. "Maybe someday you'll be married and have a nice family of your own."

"I want to get married," Moshe interjected. "I've been trying to persuade the same woman for twenty years to become frum."

"How religious is she now?" I asked.

"She lights the Shabbos candles. She keeps kosher, but that's as far as it goes."

"That's not enough?"

"That's not enough."

"Why not marry her and make her frum?"

He sighed. "It's not a possibility."

Moshe, who had earned a degree in biology at the State University of New York at Buffalo, now lived in Suffern, New

York, and worked as a mail sorter. He was typical of the educated baal tshuvas I had met who had decided that material success meant nothing to them. Yet Moshe's situation seemed more poignant than most. After two decades in the ultra-Orthodox world, he still read Hebrew at a pace so laborious that even I could keep up with him, and he ran his fingers beneath the words as he spoke them. Monsey's matchmakers had been searching for years to find him an ultra-Orthodox bride, Ahuva later told me. He was forty-seven, and suffered from a learning disability. "He has to keep running back to the rabbi and asking questions about Shabbos and the laws of Pesach. This is not what a woman wants," Ahuva said.

Moshe seemed lonely and bitter—an example, I thought, of the baal tshuva dream gone awry. My brother had been lucky in that respect: the community had provided him with a *mishpocha*—a family—and a strong sense of belonging. I tried to engage Moshe in conversation about his prospective bride in Suffern, but it only made him more hostile toward me. "Are you going to write about her in your book?" he snapped. He became voluble only when he began to discuss his pet project: in honor of Passover, he said, he had devised a telescope-like device that would allow a viewer to experience the tenth plague against the people of Egypt, described in the Torah as "a darkness that men can touch." My brother nodded approvingly—it was the kind of leisure pursuit to which he could relate.

The next day was *chol hamoed*—a day of "limited sanctity" that falls between the first and last days of a Jewish festival. Jews are permitted to drive and to work, but the holiday spirit prevails. Morah Hammer's Happy Home was closed, and even my brother had agreed to skip his daily eight hours of Talmud study at the kollel to spend the afternoon with his six children. Ahuva suggested a trip to the Bronx Zoo, but my brother's procrastination made that plan impossible. He puttered around the house, stole glances at the Talmud, burned some newly discovered chamitz in a cement pit in the backyard. By then it was nearly two o'clock—too late for an excursion into the city. Instead he proposed a drive up the thruway to the new Palisades Shopping Mall, one of the world's largest.

But there was yet another delay. First, we would have to retrieve Ahuva's station wagon from the home of Reuven, a Hasid who lived nearby. Reuven's Toyota van had broken down, and he lacked the money to have it repaired. Against the wishes of Ahuva—who viewed Reuven as hopelessly disorganized and another unhealthy influence on my brother—my brother had lent them Ahuva's car until they could find the money for repairs. When that might be, nobody knew.

Poverty seemed to be an inescapable part of my brother's world. From the signs at the Monsey Glatt Kosher Market— FOOD STAMPS AVAILABLE NOW—to the dilapidated bungalows along Blauvelt Road, one could not pass a day in Monsey without being reminded of the precarious state of most residents' lives. There were pockets of wealth, but many of Monsey's Jews were people like my brother. Struggling to support their huge families with low-paying jobs, they depended on welfare checks, food coupons, and Medicaid to get by.

My brother and Ahuva's situation was typical. Almost all of her income from Morah Hammer's Happy Home went toward paying the monthly mortgage on their home. Tuvia received a stipend of almost $300 a month from the kollel, but the monthly yeshiva tuition for the four of his children who attended school was far more than that. Insurance, house repairs, gasoline, clothing, and groceries came to another several hundred dollars a month. During the eight days of Passover, the matzoh bill alone was $300. They received monthly supplements from my mother and from Ahuva's mother. Even so, the numbers didn't add up.

Reuven, his wife, and eight children were in even worse straits. Reuven had an entrepreneurial talent, and for a while he had run a print shop in his basement, where my brother worked for two years. He had also designed Web sites for Jewish clients. Then he contracted Epstein-Barr virus, couldn't work, and lost the printing business and most of his Internet clients. He had been sick on and off for six years. His wife didn't have a job, and with eight children and no income, the family was what the community called a "Section Eight"—completely dependent on public assistance.

Ahuva shuddered as we turned into their driveway. "It just keeps getting worse," she said, surveying the broken windows of the wood-shingle house and the derelict garage filled with moldering mattresses and broken toys. In the cluttered kitchen, Reuven's wife, a baalat tshuva from Israel, was sweeping matzoh crumbs and other litter from the floor. She was a pretty woman, but she looked wan and depressed. Most of her eight small children clustered around her. With runny noses, torn clothing, and listless manners, they reminded me of some of the children I had seen in villages in Africa.

"So how was Pesach?" she asked.

"Fine, thanks."

"It's the real thing, right?"

"I've never seen anything like it."

"They call us brainwashed—but they're the ones who are brainwashed." She was speaking, I presumed, of assimilated Jews such as myself. "They don't have any idea what they're missing," she said.

I nodded politely. The smell of spoiled food, the disorder, the poor appearance of the children—all were evidence of a family in desperate need. Down in the basement, Reuven lay on a cot in an airless chamber, half covered by an old gray sheet.

Beads of sweat dappled his forehead. His beard and peyyes were damp. He seemed frail, ethereal.

"Good yom tov," he whispered, lifting his head off the pillow.

"Good yom tov," I said. "I hear you're not feeling too well."

"I have a terrible case of strep." He swallowed painfully. "Did you enjoy the seder?"

"Very much," I said.

"That's good." He handed my brother the car keys. He had spent the morning, he said, cleaning chamitz out of the car—and as a result had suffered a relapse of his fever.

With the children jammed into the rear of the station wagon, we headed north on the New York State Thruway toward the mall. A beige monolith half a mile long and five stories tall, the structure loomed over a drained swamp just off the parkway. My brother drove the station wagon carelessly through the giant parking lot, and turning a corner he almost plowed into a 1970s-era Chevrolet. The Hispanic driver mouthed obscenities through the window. My brother ignored him. "You can guess what words were coming out of his mouth," he said.

We entered the structure beside the Rain Forest Café, one of the children's favorite destinations. The mall was only half finished, and over our heads dangled heating ducts, exposed electrical cables, steel walkways, and jutting beams, like New Jersey's answer to the Pompidou Center in Paris. Ultra-Orthodox families window-shopped—enjoying a day off from work and synagogue. Ahuva carried a bag stuffed with food and beverages, including home-baked cookies, seltzer, and apples. She would not allow her children to touch the food at the mall, especially during the eight days of Pesach. Even seemingly innocuous fare such as orange juice was off limits, she explained: it might have been mixed in a vat that contained chamitz. Outside the Rain Forest Café, a crowd had gathered around an artificial jungle. Animatronic alligators, boa constrictors, and apes peered through a lush tangle of vines and banana trees. Hisses, croaks, and simian screams wafted from the plastic flora and fauna. The children—and their father—watched the display, mesmerized.

"Is this what Africa was like?" my brother asked.

"Parts of it," I said. I described a trip I had taken to the Parc National des Volcans in Rwanda, and thumped my chest in imitation of a silverback gorilla who had stared me down in the jungle.

My brother seemed as fascinated as a small child. "He never punched you?"

"Never."

"Never even took a swing at you?"

"No, he beat on his chest, then went back into the jungle."

He considered that for a moment. "Well," he said, "They're a lot tamer than the schvartzes."

I flinched but said nothing. I was still at a loss over how to deal with the most disturbing aspect of my brother's meta-morphosis: his racism. Over the years, he had hardened into an Orthodox Jewish version of our grandfather Moe, who would drive through downtown Hartford with us when we were chil-dren, muttering how the "coloreds" had brought down the neighborhood. I struggled to understand where the bigotry had come from. In part, my brother's attitudes seemed reflexive, un-thinking, a parroting of some of his rebbes in Monsey. The ultra-Orthodox Jews' historic antipathy toward African Americans— the disdain, perhaps, of one group at the margins of society for another group that it considered lower on the totem pole—went back generations, I knew. Recent events had solidified those feel-

ings of ill will, including the the Crown Heights riots of 1991—
in which a Hasidic Jew, Yankel Rosenbaum, was caught by a
mob of African American youths and stabbed to death in revenge for the hit-and-run death of a black child. My brother
sometimes cited Crown Heights as evidence that "the schvartzes
are wild people."

Biblical events gave my brother and some of his fellow
ultra-Orthodox Jews an ancient foundation for their bigotry. The
story of Ham, Noah's spiteful and jealous third son, who cas-
trated his father while the patriarch was drunk on wine and
prevented him from having a fourth son, was proof that the
blacks were pariahs, my brother once said. In the biblical account a curse was placed upon Ham by God. He would have
"swollen lips" because he spoke evil, bloodshot eyes because he
looked upon his father's nakedness, and dark skin to make him
easily identifiable. Ham, my brother maintained, sired the peoples of Africa, who were, he said, "condemned by God to be
slaves." The Africans, he said, were a godless people, lacking
"fear of heaven."

Ahuva too had no love for African Americans, telling me
how her sons had been called "Yids" and menaced by black
teenagers who lived in a housing project next to the Vin School
on the border between Spring Valley and Monsey. But my
brother's attitudes were especially intolerant. Our father, who
shared my perplexity over his son's racism, would remind me of
the words of the Book of Leviticus: "The stranger that sojourneth
with you shall be unto you as the house-born among you. And
thou shalt love him as thyself; for ye were strangers in the land
of Egypt."

My brother led his family upstairs through the half-finished structure, hurrying past Banana Republic, The Gap, Haägen-Daz,

HMV, Barnes and Noble, and other temples of conspicuous consumption. The family had the dazed looks of new arrivals on Ellis Island stupefied by the baubles of American culture. Of all the children, my brother's two oldest boys seemed the most tantalized by these glimpses of the material world. They darted in and out of shops, staring longingly at electric train sets, computer game displays, televisions, and sporting goods. Some of their friends at the Vin School were allowed to have toys. But aside from a couple of board games such as Stratego and Scrabble, my brother would not let any traces of the goy world inside his home.

His terror of secularism was the most sharply etched aspect of his personality—in part, I thought, a legacy of the Lev Tohor Rov. In his zeal to purify his nashama, he had renounced every trace of secular frivolity: sports, popular music, non-Jewish literature, the movies, theater, television. All of it weakened one's sense of the Almighty's presence in the world, he believed, and lured Jews away from their religion. American secular society was dominated by gentile culture, he said: a reminder of Jewish oppression and the *goyische* enemy. Baseball was a game that originated during the Greek exile—so why should the Jews pay homage to their former captors? When I explained to him the premise behind the television show *Seinfeld*, he likened it to Samson, shorn and abject, being trotted out to entertain the Babylonians—another Jewish clown making the goyim laugh at his own expense.

"Tateh, can I get a hockey stick for the *afikomen?*" asked Yankel, the more outgoing and self-confident of the two brothers.

"We'll see," my brother said.

"Can I get a baseball mitt?" asked Yosef Dov.

"Maybe, Yosef."

Black lace negligees bathed in lurid red light filled a Victoria's Secret window. My brother tensed, and quickened his stride. On the fourth floor, we came upon a skating rink. The boys and their older sister, Ruchel, rushed toward the rink and peered rapturously through the Plexiglas at the dozens of skaters gliding along a shimmering sheet of ice. It was a mixed crowd: teenage girls in short dresses, African Americans, Hispanics, a couple of modern Orthodox Jewish kids wearing bottle cap–sized knit yarmulkes—what Ahuva and her ultra-Orthodox friends condescendingly referred to as "Pepsi Cola *kapolehs*." The sounds of swooshing blades mingled with the gleeful cries of children and the acapella strains of "Duke of Earl."

"Can we skate, Tateh?" asked Yankel, tugging on the sleeve of his father's black overcoat.

"Not today, *kinderlach*."

The children looked crestfallen. "Please?" Yankel said.

"No." I thought I could read his mind: allowing them to skate would open the first crack in the dike. My brother, who had struggled so long and hard to free himself from the temporal realm, regarded all of his children, but especially his oldest boys, as potential defectors.

"What's wrong with it?" Ahuva demanded. It was the first time I'd seen her challenge my brother's child-rearing approach. I was inwardly elated.

"There's too much mixing," my brother said, gesturing through the smudged Plexiglas. "Those girls have exposed shoulders."

"Tuvia," she said impatiently, "have you ever been to Monsey Park? Suffern Park? Boys and girls play together there all the time. Look, there's a Satmar kid on the rink." An adolescent boy with peyyes skimmed over the ice, trailing his tsitsis.

"Just one," my brother protested.

"Tuvia, come on," I said.

I had promised myself that I would remain a disinterested observer—knowing that it was one of the conditions for my spending time with the family—but my brother's hostility toward allowing his children any normal childhood fun had pushed me over the edge.

"Tuvia," I said, "I think their nashamas will survive."

My brother glanced at me.

"Let them do it this once," Ahuva said. "Just for an hour. What harm can it do?"

"Fine," he said angrily, walking away from the skating rink. "If you want to let them go, let them go." The blame in the eyes of God, he seemed to be implying, would be hers—and mine.

"Tuvia's worried about being held accountable by Hashem when he's a hundred and twenty," she told me as my brother drifted off to sulk.

Ruchel, Yankel, and Yosef Dov ran, euphoric, to the skate rental counter. I helped them tie the laces of their black leather skates; then they hobbled up a rubber-matted ramp toward the ice on the sides of their feet. The children clutched the railing, faces tight with fear. Skaters glided past them as "It's My Party," "My Girl," and "The Wanderer" blared over the rink. Through the Plexiglas I could see my brother sitting alone in the bleachers: an incongruous figure wearing his black hat and heavy overcoat, stroking his ragged beard, lost in thought.

"Did you see me spin? Did you see me spin?" said Yosef Dov, skating up beside me, breathing heavily.

"You're heading for the Olympics, Yosef," I said.

We skated together for an hour and a half. I had never seen the children so exhilarated. I was glad for them, yet could not help thinking that I had violated an unspoken agreement with my brother. There was almost nothing that he and his wife feared more than the loss of a child to the secular world. It was nearly the equivalent of death. Some members of their community sat shivah—the seven days of ritual mourning—when a son or daughter abandoned Orthodoxy. I felt ambivalent, half hoping that his children would escape from what I often saw as the tyranny of ultra-Orthodox religion. Yet I knew that the loss of even one child would shatter my brother, and he had surely borne enough loss and anguish in his life.

At five o'clock, we found Ahuva waiting for us downstairs, beside the jungle display at the Rain Forest Café. My brother was brooding by himself on a bench beside the rest rooms.

"Are you all right?" I asked.

"I'll be fine," he muttered.

Ahuva drew me aside. "His nashama is convulsing," she said.

A few blocks from home, the children spotted a gypsy carnival. They stared longingly out the car window at the Tilt-a-Whirls and a rusty Ferris wheel. "Tateh, I want to go to the fair," said Dovid. He had been sulking since being left out of the skating adventure, and Ahuva had insisted that we find a way to cheer him up. The children began to chatter joyfully as we turned into the near-empty parking lot. Assaulted by a wave of hip-hop music, my brother winced as he stepped from the car. Suddenly, he retrieved a fistful of cassettes from his glove compartment, strode toward the fair, and had a brief exchange with the swarthy mustachioed manager. Moments later, a Yiddish folk song wafted over the fair grounds.

"What did you tell him?" I asked.

"I said, 'You want customers? Put this on instead.'"

In the penny arcade, the children scattered. Yankel took free throws at a miniature hoop, burning through the ten dollars

I gave him without scoring a basket. Ahuva took Dovid and her two youngest daughters on the Tilt-a-Whirl. My brother stopped before a ring-toss game, flanked by Ruchel and Yosef Dov. A hundred wooden pegs protruded from a board. From each peg dangled a tiny trinket—a key ring, a toy watch, a cat's-eye marble.

"Come on, Tateh," urged Ruchel.

He hesitated. Then he removed his overcoat and handed it to his daughter. He rolled up the sleeves of his white shirt, paid the tattooed barker a dollar, and, furrowing his brow with intense concentration, tossed a half dozen yellow plastic rings towards the pegs. All missed.

Leaning across the counter, flicking his wrist, he sent six more rings soaring, one after another, toward the peg board. Three scores. My brother grinned as he received the tiny prizes, then handed them to his daughter and son. He slapped another dollar bill on the counter. He rolled up his sleeves a little higher. The children compared prizes and cheered on their father.

He seemed, for a moment, like any father on an outing with his children, as he sent one ring after another spinning toward the peg board. It was the first time in eighteen years, I realized, that I had seen my brother at play.

EVERY NOW AND THEN, WHEN I WAS BACK IN New York City or Los Angeles, images from my brother's life flitted through my mind, and I was often startled by my response to them: the children clustered around him as he lit the Sabbath candles, their faces bathed half in light and half in shadow; my brother and other bearded men gathered around the Torah scrolls in the *bimah*, chanting the ancient texts as their ancestors had done through millennia; Tuvia standing alone in the back of Rabbi Meisels's synagogue, wailing kaddish, the prayer for the dead, in a bold, haunting voice; my brother and his family singing Jewish folk songs from our own Hebrew school days at the Passover table. I was no closer to giving up my agnosticism, but I could see why my brother found such comfort and safety in his world.

Even by Monsey's standards, my brother and his family lived a particularly hermetic existence. They had no newspapers, radios, televisions, or access to the Internet. My brother's only knowledge of current events came from conversations overheard in shul or while waiting in line at the Monsey Glatt Kosher Market. He voted—following the commands of Monsey's Hasidic rabbis, who usually backed the political party in power—but his attitude was that this world was irrelevant, he was passing through, biding time until the Messiah arrived.

To me, Monsey sometimes felt like a prison. The lack of privacy, the drab environment, the endless rules, the bigotry—all could be oppressive. After three or four days and nights spent standing beside my davening brother in synagogue, feasting on relentlessly heavy eastern European food, learning about the intricacies of the Torah and the Talmud, I found myself yearning for liberation, yearning to pick up a newspaper, see a movie, run around the Central Park reservoir.

In early June, after a six-week absence, I returned to Monsey for a celebration: Rabbi Moshe Meisels's son Yosef, known to everyone as Yosi, was to be married on his eighteenth birthday, in ten days' time. The bride was the daughter of an important rebbe in the Hasidic community of B'nai Brak in Israel, and the entire Meisels family—the rabbi, his wife, and their twelve other children—were planning to fly to the holy land for the wedding.

Before they left, Rabbi Meisels was throwing a feast, with dancing and music, in honor of Yosi. The guest of honor would be Grand Rabbi Mordechai Hager, the spiritual leader of the Viznitz Hasidic sect. The Viznitz rebbe made only rare excursions beyond his home and synagogue. A visit from him was, my brother said, "like having President Clinton come to eat at your house—only bigger and better." Rabbi Meisels's brother, a wealthy real estate man in Chicago, was helping to pay for the expensive affair.

My brother seemed preoccupied when I joined him for Thursday morning prayers at the Viznitz synagogue, two days before Meisels's feast. He was uncharacteristically silent as we threaded our way through a huge collection of 1970s station wagons and entered the basement of the shul for a mikvah before davening. The synagogue's stately exterior belied the grubbiness inside. Dozens of Hasidim were gathering for their morning coffee, lined up before three rusty white drums that dispensed hot water into their styrofoam cups of Folgers instant. Others scanned a bulletin board covered with advertisements for baby-sitters; rooms to rent in Monsey; cassette tape versions of the Tehillim, or Psalms of David; discount round-trip tickets to Israel. Many ultra-Orthodox living in America make pilgrimages to the holy land—but my brother wasn't one of them. He had not been back to Israel since 1981, partly because of the huge costs involved, but primarily because he felt his nashama wasn't ready for it. The Vilna Gaon, the great leader of the Litvisher Jews in eighteenth-century Lithuania, had written a famous letter while contemplating a trip to Israel in which he advised Jews to wait until their souls were utterly purified before making the journey. "I'll go there when Moshiach arrives," my brother said.

The Viznitz synagogue's mikvah was a grand-scale version of the holy bath in Meisels's basement. Naked and half-naked Hasidim bustled about the large blue-and-white-tiled room, plucking towels out of tall bins, gossiping in Yiddish on wooden benches. Pale bodies—some pudgy and pot bellied, a few strangely emaciated—filed past me on the way to the baths. Two large sacred pools, one filled with hot, the other with scalding water, were surrounded by metal guardrails and packed with bobbing bathers. Most of them stared at me as I entered the cooler of the two baths and sank beneath the water. My brother performed his usual routine: three dozen rapid dunks, eyes closed. By now I had learned that nothing in his life was performed randomly: his mikvah style was no exception. The rapid bobbing was a ritual from the Zohar—the work of Jewish mysticism from the Middle Ages that forms the basis of Kabalah. He was counting out the numerical values of Hebrew letters that spelled different names for God, he told me, and in the process learning to control different aspects of his *yetzer hara*, his evil inclination, including laziness, envy, and anger. Today, he said darkly, his main focus was on harnessing his anger.

Minutes later, after drying and ritually washing our hands, my brother and I stepped back out into the bustling basement corridor.

"Tuvia! Tuvia!"

Moshe Greenblatt, a toothsome, gangly graybeard who had known my brother for sixteen years, approached us. He and my brother made Yiddish small talk, then he turned to me.

"So?" he said.

"So?" I repeated.

"So are you rediscovering your roots?"

I could not count the number of times I had been asked a version of that question in Monsey.

"Sure."

"You live near any yeshivas in Los Angeles?"

"The Fairfax area is pretty close."

He turned to my brother. "Make sure you set him up with a Shabbos when he gets back to the West Coast." He turned back to me. "When I first met Tuvia, he wasn't even married yet," Greenblatt said. "He showed up at a wedding of one of the big rebbes, and he stood out like a sore thumb. Now he's one of the tsaddikim of Monsey." Few baal tshuvas, I was often reminded, had hurled themselves into the religious life with the energy and conviction displayed by my brother.

Down in the synagogue basement, my brother picked up his *t'fillin* from a large pile of blue and green velvet bags on a table in the hallway.

"Get me one too," I said. My longstanding reluctance to

engage in that ritual had finally begun to dissipate; I had become tired of standing idly by while all around me Jews arrayed themselves in their davening equipment.

My brother laughed. "This isn't an ice skating rink," he said. "Everybody has his own."

I stood by awkwardly while he cloaked himself in his white prayer shawl and prepared to put on his t'fillin. As if taking his own blood pressure, my brother rolled up his right sleeve, fastened one box to his right arm muscle, wrapped the black strap twice above his elbow, twirled the leather seven times below the elbow, and wrapped the remainder around his palm and fingers. Next he tied the second leather block to his forehead. As he davened in a small room with a dozen other worshipers, he pressed the box tied to his arm against his chest, forming a symbolic connection between heart and mind and God. But today his praying seemed more listless than usual. Something was clearly eating at him.

It was not until after prayers that evening that the story came spilling out of him. In front of the synagogue, after dark, my brother leaned against the door of his car and did something completely out of character. He pulled out a pack of Marlboros, lit up with trembling hands, and exhaled a cloud of smoke. I watched him, astonished. After all the talk of purifying his nashama, the sight of my brother puffing on a cigarette seemed bizarre, incongruous, and oddly uplifting. It was the first time in all the weeks we had spent together that he had let his guard slip. The aspiring tsaddik of Monsey had bad habits.

"How long have you been doing this?" I asked him.

"You want to know the truth?" he said sheepishly. "Since I was twelve. I used to sneak out of the apartment with my cigarettes, and Dad would sneak out the other door with his cigarettes."

"I mean recently."

"I started two weeks ago," he said. His wife had cornered him at the end of a long day's studying in the kollel. As part of my brother's reentry into the family after the Lev Tohor Rov episode, he would have to start behaving like the man of the house, she had told him. It was time for him to get himself together and find a decent job.

At first, my brother said, he was beside himself. Find a job? In his decade and a half in Monsey, the only full-time employment he ever had—besides managing Shlomo Helbrans's yeshiva—was in Reuven's basement print shop. Since then he had bounced through a series of ill-fated attempts to earn money. He taught English, briefly, to a class of Yiddish-speaking yeshiva boys in upstate New York. But the boys had no interest in learning English, and they taunted him mercilessly. After that debacle he and a friend went into business selling gold jewelry door to door in Rockland County, but their entire inventory—five thousand dollars' worth of bracelets and earrings—was stolen the first week. "A *potch* in the face," he called it. Next came a job selling low-flush toilets on commission to New York City landlords. That too had ended in failure.

"Every job I ever had I lost a bundle," he told me, lighting another Marlboro as the Viznitz Hasidim trickled out of synagogue. "I never had the *mazel*—the luck. I'm too trusting, I can't tell white lies." But now another opportunity was in the offing. The following Monday he was going to become a traveling salesman. A friend had hired him on a trial basis, my brother said. The friend was an ultra-Orthodox businessman from Monsey who specialized in buying "close outs"—inventories from bankrupt factories, department stores, retail shops—and reselling the goods to stores in Rockland County. Prescription drugs, computers, clothing, Swatches, exercise equipment—he traded a little of everything. Now he was seeking to expand the business.

My brother was to drive samples around the suburbs of New York and New Jersey. He would be earning commissions on everything he sold—10 percent at first, escalating to 20 percent—but no salary. In a good week, my brother had been assured, he could earn as much as a thousand dollars.

"You didn't demand a salary?"

I had a clear vision of my brother dragging around exercycles and fur coats in the back of his station wagon to minimalls in Paramus and Nyack—a Hasidic Willie Loman. I had told myself that I wouldn't get embroiled in my brother's affairs. This was between him and Ahuva. But he seemed so naive that I felt compelled to say something.

"He wasn't willing to give me a salary," he said.

"That's ridiculous."

"He doesn't know me as a salesman," he said. "He doesn't know what I can do."

Ill considered or not, there was something touching about my brother's new effort to please his wife, and the new job was just a part of it. After landing the job, he had spent two hundred dollars on a new black vest, white shirt, overcoat, *bekesher*, and fedora to replace the threadbare clothing he had been wearing for the last few years. He had hooked up his treadmill and began a daily half-hour exercise regimen. My brother was determined to look his best when he started his new job. And most strikingly, at Ahuva's insistence, he had decided to attempt a more relaxed attitude toward his children's upbringing. During the past week, he told me, he had made several trips to Pathmark in Spring Valley, bringing home hockey sticks, baseball mitts, Roller Blades, and board games including Monopoly, Life, and Uno.

"So you're okay with them playing baseball now?"

"No comment."

The whole process, he admitted after a pause, was filling his soul with *agmas nefesh*. For the sake of his marriage, he was planning to reduce his Talmudic studies from eight hours to one or two hours a day, curtail the time he spent davening, and abandon his dreams of sending his boys to a Hasidic yeshiva. Everything the Lev Tohor Rov had taught him about absolute devotion to God, about upgegebenkeit, would have to be moderated. He was smoking a pack of Marlboros a day to calm his nerves. Rabbi Meisels, a chain smoker himself, had reassured him that it was all right. "Don't worry about this," he'd said. "In certain times of stress it's excusable. You're taking on a new job, a new life."

As we drove back to the house from the Viznitz synagogue, my brother stuffed his mouth with spearmint chewing gum, but he could not disguise the odor that permeated his clothing. Ahuva detected it the moment we walked in the living room. Her nostrils flared, her eyes narrowed. She looked at him accusingly, then at me. "Who's been smoking?"

My brother and I eyed each other nervously, like guilty schoolchildren caught lighting up in the boys' room.

"Who's been smoking?" she asked again. "I didn't know you smoked," she said to me. I nodded across the room at my brother.

"I can't believe you're smoking, Tuvia," she said. "I'm allergic to that smell. It's disgusting." She threw the windows open, fanned the air, then fled to her bedroom and slammed the door. He watched her go. "She's strong, isn't she?" he said, half in admiration, I thought, and half in fear.

But the Lev Tohor Rov had not completely disappeared from my brother's life. The next morning a Toyota minivan pulled alongside us as we walked back up the hill toward home from the Viznitz synagogue. I recognized the peyyes-wearing driver as Uri Goldman, the ex-Israeli soldier who ran Rabbi Helbrans's yeshiva. A quartet of the rabbi's acolytes sat jammed in the back—like Hasidic henchmen. Goldman nodded in greeting, then he and my brother huddled for several minutes, murmuring in Yiddish.

"*Yasher koach*," he said to Goldman as the van drove away. Go with strength. He looked concerned.

"What's going on with the Lev Tohor Rov?"

"It's a bad situation," he said. Three years ago, surgeons at the prison hospital had operated on the Lev Tohor Rov for a hernia, but the medical care was poor. They were "shoemakers," my brother said, not doctors. The hernia had come back—bleeding, growing larger, protruding from his abdomen—and needed to be operated on fast. But the Lev Tohor Rov had no health insurance, and he was deeply in debt. The contributions from Hasidic supporters had dried up in recent months. He owed fifty thousand dollars to the attorney handling his deportation case. Even the yeshiva was on the verge of collapse. The students, few of whom had green cards and could not earn any money legally in the United States, were scrounging for small loans just to feed themselves. Though financially squeezed himself, my brother was secretly writing checks for fifty, a hundred dollars to help them out from time to time. "Now, on top of everything else, they can't find a doctor willing to do the operation," he told me. Goldman had asked him to help them find a surgeon. Ahuva insisted that he have no further contact with the rabbi or his followers. But what was he supposed to do? he asked. Sit back while the Lev Tohor Rov got sicker?

After his release from jail in November 1996, the Lev Tohor Rov had made a critical misjudgment. Two young Hasidic men from upstate New York had run away from a community led by their grandfather, a highly respected rebbe, and joined Shlomo Helbrans's sect in Monsey. The rebbe had denounced the Lev Tohor Rov, my brother said, and the community launched a "propaganda war" against him. Familiar allegations swirled: that the rabbi had prevented the young men's families from having any contact with them; he had brainwashed them to turn against their grandfather. Now Helbrans was a pariah. One Hasidic community after another had turned away from him. In Monsey he could no longer walk the streets without facing abuse. I found the rabbi's fall from grace ironic. "So it's all right if a non-observant Jewish kid is kidnapped, but when it happens to one of their own kind, there's a stink?" I asked.

"That's the way it works," he said. "These sorts of disputes happen all the time in this community."

The Lev Tohor Rov still had one major backer: the Skvira rebbe, the charismatic, fiercely anti-Zionist head of the village of New Square, three miles from Monsey. But the Skvira rebbe was facing his own money problems, millions of dollars in fines relating to an alleged scam against the federal government. Sect leaders had allegedly "enrolled" thousands of phony students into Judaism courses at Rockland County Community College between 1986 and 1991, and collected twenty million dollars in federal tuition grants. Six Hasidim—including New Square's mayor—had been indicted for fraud. FBI and IRS agents were still hunting down residents to issue them subpoenas. The Skvira rebbe was struggling to keep his community afloat, and had nothing left for the Lev Tohor Rov. "There's talk that the Skvira rebbe has lost control," Tuvia admitted. "He's assured people that nobody will go to prison for this, but the community is in trouble. They don't have much to begin with, and now they're hit with these multimillion-dollar fines."

My brother was ambivalent about the scandal. "Do you think they're using the money to take trips to the Riviera?" he asked. "Buy a summer house on Martha's Vineyard? The money is going to feed families at Shabbos, to help the handicapped." But the notion that Hasidim could be just as dishonest as anyone else was clearly a grave embarrassment for him. When I pressed him for more details, he quickly changed the subject.

My brother's pained efforts to wean himself from Shlomo Helbrans continued, in fits and starts. After school on Friday, Yosef Dov had organized a softball game in Manny Weldler Park at the edge of Monsey. He was bringing his new baseball glove— and Ahuva insisted that my brother make an appearance to cheer him on.

On a bright, sunny afternoon we pulled into the parking lot beside the baseball fields in the large public park. Yosef Dov was already there, trying to regiment thirty boys who milled about a neatly manicured diamond. He waved to us excitedly as we settled onto the grass behind the third base line. It was a curious sight. All the boys wore yarmulkes; most had tsitsis dangling from beneath their shirts, only a handful wore baseball mitts. Nobody appeared to have the slightest idea how to play the game. A half dozen boys sat in the outfield, another twelve drifted about the infield. There were four first basemen, three shortstops. Yosef Dov was pitching. He fired the softball overhand at a bespectacled catcher who squatted, without a face mask, a few inches behind the batter. A foul tip struck the catcher squarely in the glasses, shattering them with a sickening crack.

I winced as the boy stared uncomprehendingly at his broken lenses. My brother was oblivious. He sat on the grass, flanked by his son Dovid and his daughter Gnendi, who munched happily on animal crackers. He was reading from a prayer book, looking up from time to time to scowl at the raucous cheers of the players.

"This is giving me a lot of agmas nefesh," my brother muttered. "I can't tell you how much agmas nefesh this gives me." Tuvia had sought advice from Rabbi Meisels on how to handle his sons' enthusiasm for athletics. He worried that competition for temporal rewards bred jealousy, rivalry, ambition, and greed. Worse, he feared that baseball would distract them from the study of the Talmud. Meisels had struck a moderate tone. "Don't worry about it, Tuvia," he said. "My uncle was a star soccer player in his village in Hungary. He became a *groise* rabbi in America."

But his doubts had not been assuaged. The situations were different, he told me. "Meisels's uncle grew up before the war in eastern Europe, in a shtetl with a rabbi on every block. A person could play soccer and still be immersed in yiddishkeit." Besides, soccer was one thing—baseball something else. "All this screaming and yelling," he said. "It hurts my nashama just to listen to it."

"Don't you view athletic grace as a testament to the greatness of Hashem?" I asked him.

He shook his head. "Screaming and yelling on a baseball diamond, or sitting in the stands with twenty-five thousand goyim, watching them guzzle beer while another goy hits a ball four hundred feet? This is not for us."

I remembered my brother's love of sports in his youth. Before enrolling in the High School of Performing Arts, he had been a tennis player, a shortstop at summer camp, and an avid Boston Red Sox fan in the days of Carl Yastrzemski and Tony Conigliaro. My brother and I would take the bus down from Riverdale to watch the Yankees play the Red Sox during the hot Bronx summers of the early 1970s, buying general admission tickets and then sneaking past the ushers into box seats behind the first or third base lines. Over hot dogs and Cokes, I would teach him how to keep score, and we would argue over the relative merits of Thurman Munson versus Carlton Fisk, Mel Stottlemyre versus Jim Lonborg. Now it was as if my brother were fighting a constant battle to negate that part of himself, as if the joy he once had derived from sports was a dangerous sensation that had to be suppressed.

· · ·

By nine-thirty on Saturday night, every window of Rabbi Mei-sels's house was illuminated. The engagement party was begin-ning, and station wagons and taxis disgorged a stream of Hasidim in front of the synagogue. Everyone was excited, everyone wait-ing for the arrival of the Viznitz rebbe. My brother too was cheer-ful. The problems of the Lev Tohor Rov, which had been weighing heavily on him all week, seemed to have been rele-gated to the background as he prepared to share in his friend's joy. After years of being shunted aside by Helbrans, Rabbi Mei-sels had become an integral part of my brother's life again.

Inside the basement shul the mood was festive. White ban-ners festooned the walls, proclaiming, in Hebrew, "Love and Delight Shall Fill the Tents of Tsaddikim." A klezmer band—clarinetist, keyboardist, and drummer—at the front of the syn-agogue played a polka-like tune, and young male waiters laid out heaping trays of almond cakes, coconut cakes, potato kugel, kid-ney beans, and cole slaw. Rabbi Meisels held court behind a table that ran the length of his basement synagogue, looking like a resplendent walrus in a shiny black jacket, streimel, breeches, and white cotton knee socks. Seventeen-year-old Yosi, a fresh-faced boy with a wispy goatee and thin mustache, sat beside him, gazing out dazedly from underneath his streimel. He accepted the congratulations of a stream of well-wishers with an uncom-fortable smile, as if the whole event were not his idea. He seemed awfully young to be getting married.

"Has he ever met the bride?" I asked my brother.

"Once—in Israel," my brother replied.

The waiters—strapping young men wearing jeans, sneakers, and little terry cloth yarmulkes over their mops of curly hair—had the ruggedly handsome look of kibbutzniks. They were mod-ern Orthodox Jews, employees of a catering service that Meisels sometimes used, and my brother was a little discomfited by their presence here. Although the modern Orthodox Jews ranked far higher in his estimation than the Reform Jews, who did not even keep kosher, they were still too attached to the secular world, he said, to come close to God. The clothes they wore betrayed the heavy influence of American culture; many attended Yeshiva University, where they were indoctrinated in sciences, literature, and other secular subjects. They read *The New York Times*, listened to baseball and basketball games, owned televisions. It saddened him. "When we see someone like this we feel like we're looking at a baseball player with fantastic tools who's playing in the Little League," he told me. "He's wasting his gifts as a Yid."

A murmur shot through the crowd. Flanked by a dozen yeshiva boys and secretaries, the Viznitz rebbe strode imperially into the synagogue. He was a stout man in his seventies. Large horn-rimmed glasses and dark beetle brows accentuated his owlish visage. The Hasidim clustered around him joyfully. Yeshiva boys jumped up and down in excitement. The Viznitz rebbe sat down stiffly beside Rabbi Meisels. Their huge hats collided. He sipped from a silver goblet of wine and nibbled on a piece of challah bread. A clean-shaven, curly-haired waiter in Nike sneakers and jeans presented him with a glistening salmon. He picked at it reflectively, sitting back to chew, observing the crowd with hands folded across his chest.

My brother found the Viznitz rebbe stern and intimidating—but he would often speak in awe of the rebbe's *kadusha*, or holiness. He was the type of man, my brother said, who over-salted his food intentionally just to spoil the taste of it, because he believed that earthly appetites distracted one from contemplation of the world to come. He was a proud leader who, I had learned, jealously guarded his stature as the biggest macher in Monsey. Three years earlier members of a different sect—the Satmars—dared to install a siren on their synagogue roof to summon the faithful to prayer. It was in direct competition with the siren on top of the Viznitz synagogue. The Viznitz rebbe had used his influence with Ramapo town officials to have the installers fined for violating a building code. He was also uncompromising in his faith. Recently, my brother told me, the Viznitz rebbe had been greeted by one of his wealthiest contributors outside the eirev on a Saturday morning. Noticing that the man was wearing a gold watch, in violation of Sabbath rules, the rebbe had refused to shake his hand. The donor had become so irate at the snub that he announced he would no longer give money to the Viznitz synagogue. When the Viznitz rebbe received word of the man's actions, he was said to have replied, "Good riddance."

The rebbe's secretaries pushed aside tables and cleared a space in the center of the room. The rebbe rose, took Yosi by the hand, and led him to the floor. Their hands clasped together, they waltzed slowly about the synagogue. The Viznitz rebbe's eyes were tightly shut. Yosi stared straight ahead of him, trance-like, his face frozen into a smile. Rabbi Meisels soon joined them, followed by half a dozen others who held hands and danced in a tight circle. Suddenly, a commotion erupted directly behind my table: a dozen Hasidic women wearing floral ankle-length dresses and head scarfs began pushing excitedly against the white wood screen that separated them from the men, hoping for a glimpse of the dancing Viznitz rebbe. "Move it," they shouted. "Get down! We can't see!"

Poor Yosi, I thought. It must have been difficult for him. He was seventeen years old, about to marry a girl he had met once in his life, saddled with the enormous expectations of the entire Viznitz community, including those of the Viznitz rebbe himself. What would happen to Yosi, I wondered, if the marriage didn't work out? The divorce rate among even the most isolated Jewish sects had soared in recent years. Ahuva guessed that as many as 20 percent of marriages among the ultra-Orthodox in Monsey now ended in a get, compared with 5 or 10 percent when she had first arrived in the community fifteen years earlier.

The rebbe finished one dance and then immediately bustled out the door of the synagogue, followed by his entourage. His visit to Bais Iyel had lasted a grand total of fifteen minutes. A waiter came in bearing a plate of kugel for him. "It's too late," Rabbi Meisels said forlornly. "He's already gone."

The waiter looked surprised. "That was fast."

"Why did he leave so quickly?" I asked my brother.

"Why should he stay around? What's he going to do, smoke a cigarette? Make small talk? He honors Yosi by his brief presence."

My brother looked haggard the next morning when I climbed up the steep stairs from my clammy basement bedroom and stumbled into him in the kitchen of his house. He had been unable to sleep all night, he told me as he stirred himself a cup of instant coffee and said a barucha. The party at Meisels's shul had been a distraction, but now that it was over, he was back to brooding about his new job, which was scheduled to start at eight o'clock on Tuesday morning. He was wavering, thinking of calling in sick. Maybe he would resign before he even started. He was not sure he had the mazel for this type of work, he said. Moreover, he was not sure he was willing to reduce his Talmudic study so drastically. He had decided to consult a rebbe known as the Rachman Strivka that evening in Borough Park, Brooklyn. He invited me to join him.

I was losing count of all the rebbes in my brother's orbit. There was the Viznitz rebbe and the Skvira rebbe. There was also the Satmar rebbe and the Tosh rebbe. Most Hasidim have just one spiritual leader whom they revere as a conduit to God.

But my brother was a sort of Hasidic free agent, attending the tish in different synagogues, seeking blessings and advice from a half dozen rebbes. The Rachman Strivka in Borough Park—a brother-in-law to both the Viznitz and the Skvira rebbes—was the one to whom he confided his most personal problems. He and Ahuva had sought the Rachman Strivka's advice several times during the rockiest periods of their marriage.

At ten o'clock that night, we sped down Lexington Avenue in the aging Mercury on our way to Brooklyn. The car had the stale, musty smell of cigarette smoke—and the ashtray, I noticed, was now filled with butts. I pointed out our old apartment building on the corner of Lexington and Eightieth Street, the coffee shop where we had been eating dinner with our parents when a radio bulletin announced that Martin Luther King Jr. had been shot. Passing through the old neighborhood again brought a wave of conflicting emotions. It made me feel at once closer to my brother—and irretrievably far away. Turning toward the FDR Drive on Seventy-second Street, we passed Temple Shaaray Tefila—a white windowless cube that dominated the southwest corner of First Avenue.

"You remember this church?" he asked me. He had an edge in his voice. I sensed another jeremiad coming on.

"Sure I do," I said. "I was bar mitzvahed there."

"You gave an angry speech against the Vietnam War."

"It was June 1970—a couple of weeks after Kent State."

"Teddy Roosevelt would have known how to deal with those demonstrators."

My brother's non sequitur startled me. "What do you mean?"

"He would have taken a hard line."

"The governor of Ohio sent out the National Guard and killed four of them," I said. "What do you call that?"

"I'm just saying there's a weakness of leaders these days." My brother's political conservatism never failed to surprise me when I remembered the radical college student I had known.

"It's the same in the Jewish world," he continued. "We're down to a handful of tsaddikim. It's a difficult time. And now we've got these people"—he gestured to the Reform temple—"to contend with." I braced myself for another lecture.

"Even the goyim's churches are closer to the truth," he said. "At least they recognize that there's an Almighty. These Reform people—believing what they want to believe, doing what they want to do. They're rebels in Hashem's kingdom."

Nearing Borough Park, we drove through a poorer neighborhood, populated mostly by African Americans. My brother rolled up the windows. "Blacks and Jews always live side by side," he said. "Do you know why?"

"Why?"

"Because the Jews suck up all the *kadisha* from a place. In the vacuum, the lower elements move in." I sighed, saying nothing.

The Rachman Strivka led a Hasidic community of five hundred adherents scattered throughout Brooklyn and beyond. His prayers were believed to be "readily accepted by heaven," my brother told me, so he was highly popular among ultra-Orthodox Jews of all sects. After the evening prayer, the Rachman Strivka made himself available in his office to anyone who wished to speak with him. The appointments were on a first-come, first-served basis, and limited to ten minutes each.

We parked the car in a tidy tree-lined neighborhood of town houses and small apartment blocks in the heart of Borough Park, now home to about ninety thousand Hasidim. Evening prayer services were just ending when we arrived at the rebbe's synagogue. My brother paced the sidewalk in front as the Hasidim began streaming out, and lit another Marlboro. "This is one of the things I've got to talk to the Rachman Strivka about," he said.

The rebbe—a gnomish septuagenarian with long gray beard and bulbous red nose—sat at the far end of an oak table covered with prayer books. He was an avuncular man, lacking the unnerving intensity of the Lev Tohor Rov. He smiled warmly at me, and I wished him "Shalom aleichem."

"My brother is a big journalism macher from Los Angeles," my brother told him in Yiddish, the only language the rebbe spoke, although he had lived in Brooklyn for decades. The Rachman Strivka mumbled something in a nasal voice. My brother seemed a little embarrassed.

"He wants to know if you're married."

He turned back to the rebbe. "He's not married," he said. "We're hoping to find him an *ehrliche*—God-fearing—woman."

The Rachman Strivka said something else. My brother laughed.

"What's he saying, Tuvia?" I asked.

"He says that during the era of the Second Temple, when the princes wanted to make an offering to Hashem, they brought spoons that were then melted down to make five ounces of gold."

"Spoons?"

"The message is, 'With just a small spoonful of effort, you can become a golden Jew.'"

Again I was reminded of how our roles had been reversed in his world. My brother was the "golden Jew"; I was the errant sibling, viewed as a potential returnee. I was the one who did not measure up.

My brother asked me to leave the room so he could consult with the rebbe privately. When he emerged ten minutes later, he seemed relieved.

"Everything okay?"

"Baruch Hashem," he said. My brother had told the rebbe

that he was having second thoughts about the job. The rebbe had been understanding but firm. "You have to give it a try," he said. "You need to earn money for your family, for your children. If Hashem decides it's not right for you, he'll let you know."

"But the fire in my belly has dimmed. I'm smoking, schmoozing, studying the Talmud less," my brother remonstrated.

"So?" said the rebbe. "The Almighty gives Jews tests all the time. It's easy to study the Torah when one is filled with desire. But it's during the time when desire is wanting that Hashem puts a man to the test."

"Rebbe," Tuvia said. "Sometimes I'm a little down. What am I supposed to do about it?"

"You can be down," the rebbe told him. "But don't bring it into the house. It's a mitzvah to be *samayach*—happy—and an even bigger mitzvah to pretend to be *samayach*."

We drove home along the Brooklyn-Queens Expressway beneath a star-filled summer sky. I enjoyed these moments with my brother—the intimacy of the automobile, the sense of having journeyed into the hidden corners of his world. Borough Park had struck me as one of the more congenial aspects of my brother's life. The Rachman Strivka seemed a voice of moderation, and if he was helping to guide my brother back to his family, then I could have nothing but positive feelings toward him.

The illuminated towers of lower Manhattan and the Brooklyn Bridge were spread out before us like Oz: a dazzling contrast to the world we had left behind in Borough Park. This vibrant panorama proclaimed a world of money, ambition, power, the energy of human industry. I wondered whether my brother was feeling a twinge of yearning as he confronted these glittering secular playgrounds where he had spent a good part of his youth.

"This never fails to amaze me every time I see it," I said as we rumbled onto the bridge.

"Those who adore Hashem are heading for a place where the intensity and brightness is a hundred thousand times greater than this," he said. This time the words struck me as rote, delivered without his usual passion.

"Did you ever think where you might be if you hadn't gone into this life?" I asked him, gazing through the web of steel cables toward the flickering lights of boats plying the East River, and the stream of traffic hurtling along the FDR Drive.

"I thought about it. I'd be a waiter in Greenwich Village, waiting to see my name in lights."

"Maybe your name would have been in lights."

"And my nashama would have been in darkness. Where's Frank Sinatra now?"

"He's dead."

"But a Jew lives and lives and lives."

I felt a wave of sympathy for him as I imagined him embarking on this new phase in his life. Tuesday, I imagined, would be a difficult day. I pictured him trundling his samples across Rockland County, facing the stony stares of street-smart merchants—trying to get by on the proverbial smile and a shoeshine. I wanted him to succeed. I wanted him to sell those exercise machines and Swatches, to rake in commissions, to buy his children and his wife everything they yearned for. Almost without realizing it, I had become caught up in the small dramas of his life.

"Good luck, Tuvia," I said as he dropped me in front of our father's apartment.

"*Zeit gezundt,*" he said. I stood on the sidewalk, beneath the green awning, and watched him drive off in his Marquis toward the West Side Highway.

ONE EVENING IN JULY, I CALLED MONSEY
from Juneau, Alaska, on my way home to Los Angeles
from a long reporting assignment in the Alaskan interior.
I had not spoken with my brother in more than a month,
and I was anxious to find out how he was faring in his
new job. New York was in the grip of a mid-summer heat
wave, and Ahuva sounded envious when I told her where
I was calling from.

"Oy," she said. "Life is turned upside down again.
The kids are all off to summer camp. We just packed
Ruchel off this morning."

"How's Tuvia's job working out?"

"Which job? He's lost two of them the last month."

My heart sank. "You're kidding."

"He didn't even start them. They both fell through."

"Both of them?" The long weeks of agonizing about
his nashama, the trip to Brooklyn to see the Rachman
Strivka—all for naught. My brother seemed more luckless
than ever. "Are there any new prospects?"

"I made Tuvia take a computer programming aptitude test," Ahuva said.

"Computer programming?" It sounded dismal. I imagined Ahuva tearing off one of those forms from a poster on the New York City subway, next to the advertisements for laser surgery. You can change your life with one phone call. Dial 1-800-COMPUTE.

"The guy who administered the test couldn't believe it. Tuvia did so well that they wanted him to start the training course immediately."

"Is he doing it?"

"He's already started. We took out a loan to pay the tuition. It costs seven thousand dollars. Baruch Hashem, we'll manage. Then Tuvia will finish the course in January and he'll be able to find a better job. By February he'll be out in the job market."

"That sounds good," I said doubtfully.

"Tuvia is working so hard on the marriage," Ahuva said, confiding in me with a directness that I had not expected. "He wants to give me things—like a diamond ring—and right now he can't, so he's motivated to succeed. But it's a difficult time. Just the car fare is costing him two hundred dollars a month. This winter when Shabbos starts at four o'clock I'll be lucky to get him in the door by three-thirty. But hopefully by the end it will all be worth it."

"He sounds like he's changed a lot."

"You wouldn't even recognize him."

My brother came to the phone a minute later. He had been davening in the basement. "Hello, big brother," he said, sounding ebullient. He hadn't called me that in decades. "How are things in California?"

"I'm in Alaska," I said.

"Alaska? Oy vey, are you looking for the lost tribe?"

"You mean the Eskimos?"

"I don't think so, unless that fur hood on their heads is a yarmulke."

"How about the sales job? Ahuva told me it didn't work out."

"It couldn't be helped. He's opening a new business, he's got two new retail stores in the Catskills, and he's overextended. The day before I was supposed to start, he told me he needed to wait and see how things were going."

"Were you disappointed?"

"I wasn't disappointed. Computers are better for me. You can make sixty, seventy thousand dollars in a year."

It seemed like another one of my brother's pipe dreams— but I wanted to encourage him. "You're starting to sound like a real businessman."

He laughed. "A man has to support his family," he said.

We met up at the Monsey Trails bus stop on West Forty-first Street and Broadway on a sticky Thursday afternoon in early August. Midtown Manhattan seemed airless. People walked through the steamy canyons listlessly, drenched in sweat, some holding umbrellas against the brutal sun. I drifted along Broadway in the ninety-degree heat, searching for the Monsey Trails sign, my temples pounding, nearly overcome by a noxious combination of car exhaust and greasy fast-food smells. Times Square, which had just reopened following a fatal accident at the Condé Nast construction site, was the last place I wanted to be at the height of summer.

I had come east to join my brother and his family for Tisha B'Av, the Jewish day of mourning for the destruction of the First and Second Temples in Jerusalem. Tradition holds that, throughout history, calamities always befell Jews on the eighth day of the month of Av, when the Almighty abandoned his chosen people. Tisha B'Av seemed to be the counterpoint to all the other yom tovs I had spent with my brother and his family. Those festivals always seemed to fall on brisk, clear days and were happy occasions, celebrations of God's miracles and his covenant with the Jewish people. Tisha B'Av was sad and oppressive, and the torpid August weather seemed appropriate.

For twenty-one days leading up to Tisha B'Av, Jews must refrain from singing, dancing, washing clothing, or bathing—a particularly onerous prohibition at the height of the New York summer. For the last nine days the prohibitions intensify—no eating of meat, no shaving. No marriages can take place, or expressions of joy. Jews must fast on the day of mourning, and in the evening they flock to shul wearing slippers or sneakers— leather shoes are discarded because they're regarded as a symbol of comfort—to sit on the floor, wail for the loss of the Temple, and pray for a speedy end to their exile.

My brother waited with three other ultra-Orthodox commuters on the northwest corner of Forty-first Street and Broadway, clutching a leather briefcase. All of them were perspiring heavily beneath their layers of thick black clothing. "Shalom aleichem, Yehoshua," he said. He eyed my bare scalp. "Did you bring a kipa?" I slapped the yarmulke on my head obediently. My head throbbed from the heat and sunlight. I purchased a can of Diet Coke from a street vendor and popped open the lid while we waited for the bus.

"Say a *shehakol*," my brother reminded me. Again, I did as I was told, muttering the words by rote. I had been in my brother's company so often by this time, I realized, that reciting an ancient Hebrew blessing over a can of Coke on a sizzling street corner in Midtown Manhattan now seemed perfectly natural to me.

My brother seemed drained yet upbeat. Three weeks into

the programming course, he was discovering that he actually enjoyed working with computers, he told me as we boarded the bus back home.

"It's like learning Russian," he said, showing me his textbook.

I dried my sweaty forehead with a tissue and leafed through page after page of rune-like C language, as impenetrable to me as the Hebrew texts of the Talmud. "I thought you were like me—no aptitude for this stuff."

"I have no aptitude for it," he said. "But I have to feed my children."

His schedule was grueling. He woke up at five-thirty in the morning Monday through Friday, studied Talmud for an hour with another scholar at Meisels's shul, then bathed in the mikvah to "inoculate" himself before commuting to Manhattan. He ate breakfast aboard the seven-fifteen minyan bus—a special prayer bus reserved for men—and davened all the way into the city. At nine o'clock he arrived in his classroom on William Street in lower Manhattan.

At first, he told me, he had not been certain whether his nashama could withstand the changes of his new life. They had put him in a classroom with women, *chas v'shalom*—God forbid. Nonreligious women. My brother and another student, a Russian Jewish immigrant, had complained about it, and the director of the school had agreed to set up an extra class for men only. Now all the students in his class were ultra-Orthodox Jews, and his teacher, by an auspicious coincidence, was the brother-in-law of a close Hasidic friend from Monsey.

"So you see? The Abeshter is looking out for me," he said. "If I can keep my mind on Hashem even while I work, and not think that I'm going to be the best in the class, and win awards, and be a programming genius, I'll be all right."

"Are you still smoking?"

"Not as much as before. I've gotten over the worst of it, baruch Hashem."

Computer programming was not the kind of career I once would have envisioned for my brother, the former actor, campaign manager, and philosophy major. Punching keys in some drab building in lower Manhattan was only slightly less bleak, I thought, than selling close-out merchandise from the back of a beat-up station wagon. Even if he managed to stick with the seven-month course, there was no guarantee that he would be able to find a job. Yet I realized what a significant step this was. My brother, it appeared, had finally broken free of the Lev Tohor Rov. He was making a serious effort to reconcile the demands of his God and the needs of his family. It was a breakthrough, and I was exhilarated to see it.

We reached Monsey at five o'clock. In the August heat my brother's neighborhood seemed even scruffier than usual. Many people were away, vacationing in the Catskills. The Viznitz rebbe had taken most of his flock with him to Gibbers, a yeshiva camp in the mountains. Hasidim in sweat-stained white shirts stood before their dirty wood-shingle bungalows, watering parched brown lawns. My brother took it all in and sighed with relief.

"It's wonderful coming back here," he said.

"I know. Summer in the city can be awful."

"It's not the trees or the grass. It's the Yiddin. It's being surrounded by Yiddin."

Tentatively, my brother was reconnecting with the world beyond the borders of his community for the first time since he had embraced yeshiva life sixteen years earlier. And the programming course was just a part of it. Minutes after returning home, my brother called me into his bedroom and opened a new mahogany cabinet at the foot of his bed. I looked on, dumbstruck. A new IBM desktop computer with a high-definition nineteen-inch screen, 56,000-baud modem, and a Toshiba laser printer gleamed on the cabinet shelf. I felt almost the way I had when my brother pulled out his Marlboros in front of the Viznitz synagogue. It was an utterly unexpected side of my brother—a dimension that I'd figured had vanished long ago.

"When did you get this?"

"Last month," my brother said, grinning.

"You have Internet access?"

"I'm a subscriber to America Online."

"America Online?" I was amazed. The computer, he explained, had been a gift from Mitchell and our mother to my brother's children. Ahuva had persuaded him to allow them to play computer games—but it was my brother, not the kids, who had become hooked. Last week he had opened up an e-mail account. He was cruising the Internet every evening after work. A window into secular society had been opened and, astonishingly, my brother couldn't seem to get enough of it. I watched over his shoulder as he booted up the computer and dialed into his Internet server. Effortlessly wielding the mouse, he scanned the day's news—paying particular attention to a report about the president's impending appearance before a grand jury investigating his relationship with Monica Lewinsky.

"Clinton should just come clean with the American people," my brother pronounced. "He should tell them that he was a bad husband, that he let his daughter down and let Hillary down."

"That'll never happen unless they find something on the dress."

He spat in disgust. Back to the familiar Tuvia. Direct sexual references always provoked that response in my brother. It was a traditional Jewish method of repelling evil words or thoughts. But then he launched into a Talmudic interpretation of the relationship between president and intern. "The fact is, he really hasn't done anything wrong," he said. "There's nothing in the Torah that forbids a man—especially a goy—having relations with a woman other than his wife as long as the other woman isn't married."

I realized I still had a lot to learn about Jewish law—but somehow I was encouraged at my brother's newfound interest in the outside world. Two months ago, he had immediately changed the subject when I asked him his thoughts about the Lewinsky affair. For better or worse, he now seemed captivated by the morality play in Washington.

Later that evening, while my brother went to the mikvah, Ahuva brewed a pot of tea in the kitchen and shared with me her thoughts about the new direction in her husband's life. They were struggling financially now, she admitted, even more than when Tuvia was working—without pay—for the Lev Tohor Rov. They had taken out the loan to pay for the computer course, borrowed more to send Ruchel and Yosef Dov to summer camp in the Catskills—and had no income besides a few dollars Ahuva was earning from summer tutoring. She was scanning the Internet for on-line auctions of cheap clothing. The kitchen was filled with cases of sweet kosher pickles and sugary cereals—a summer handout of surplus groceries to needy families made by a local yeshiva. I had made a few efforts to help them in the past, but my brother—out of pride—had always rejected them.

Yet Ahuva didn't really seem depressed by their penury. What was important, she said, was that her husband had his feet on the ground again. "Tuvia will find a good job. Maybe he'll earn forty-five thousand a year, and we can get off Uncle Sam's medical insurance and get on some job-related plan," she told me. "His dream is to buy me a one-carat diamond ring for ten thousand. I never received an engagement ring. I told him not to worry about it. But he's got the idea in his head."

After the reserve of our first encounters, Ahuva had warmed toward me considerably. I sensed that she welcomed having someone to talk to who knew her husband well. She made no secret about how distant and uncommunicative he could be, how wrapped up he was in his own spiritual improvement. For a brief time a few years back, when my brother had helped Ahuva run Morah Hammer's Happy Home, it had been wonderful, she said; they had had a common purpose, they were talking all the time, the relationship had flourished. But then "a certain rabbi" in Monsey—not Shlomo Helbrans—had told my brother to quit. It was undignified, the rabbi said, for a Jew to work for his wife. They had lost the bond that had been forged by teaching together, and had never really recovered it.

Ahuva, I thought, sensed my concern for my brother's welfare. Over time my brother seemed to have become our joint project, and these conversations in the kitchen had taken on the feeling of progress reports. The warming up was mutual. I found myself admiring her more each time I saw her. She was the opposite of the stereotype of the Orthodox Jewish wife— meek, utterly subservient to the demands of her husband. In my eyes she had rescued my brother, and I could not imagine where he would be had she walked out of the marriage, leaving him to fend for himself.

"Is he still speaking to the Lev Tohor Rov?" I asked her.

"I'd give it to him if he tried," she said, handing me a cup of tea. "The other day the Lev Tohor Rov's secretary called, asking for help with his computer. He wanted Tuvia's beeper number. I told him I don't give out the number to just anybody. Later he saw Tuvia at the mikvah and complained. When Tuvia came home, he asked me why I was so rude."

She creased up her face in distaste. "Even the kids are

pulling away from that man now. Last week Yankel saw a Hasidic boy from Lev Tohor Rov's yeshiva at the mikvah. And he said, 'You're still over there? What a pity.'"

"Yankel is taking after you," I noted.

"Tuvia's changing. Have you noticed that he's wearing a short suit jacket? Before he was wearing one down below his knees, Hasidic style. I told him, 'Tuvia, we don't match. I feel uncomfortable walking down the street with you.' Tuvia said that I was trying to stop him from expressing himself. But the next morning he wore the short jacket to work."

There had been setbacks, she conceded. Weeks ago Rabbi Meisels had returned from Yosi's wedding in Israel, filled with religious fire. During prayers "he was shouting, shaking all over the place," Ahuva recalled. "Yosef Dov saw his father davening with Meisels in the same way, and he ran out of shul." I pictured Yosef Dov watching in embarrassment as his father convulsed like a madman. The children had never revealed to me their feelings about the Lev Tohor Rov—and I had not dared bring up the subject. But now I understood how difficult it must have been for them to witness their father's transformation. "He saw Tuvia reverting back to the way he used to be," Ahuva continued. "Tuvia said, 'I'll daven any way I like. If my son doesn't like it, that's too bad.' I said, 'Tuvia, what does it matter if you lose fifty calories or a thousand calories when you're davening?' Tuvia grumbled, but he agreed to tone it down."

"It must be painful for him," I said.

"The way I look at it, Tuvia is going through a delayed adolescence. I told him, 'You've been a frum Jew for sixteen years. When Raizel Weiss's boys were sixteen, they were just like you—extremists. 'Oy, did that make him furious. 'How can you say that?' he said. 'You make me sound like a child.'"

Ahuva's explanation for my brother's behavior struck me as somewhat simplistic—perhaps as wishful thinking. His tendency toward fanaticism seemed not a passing phase, I thought, but rather a fundamental part of his character. My brother may have removed himself physically from the Lev Tohor Rov's domain, but, I sensed, he would never be able to truly separate himself from the rabbi's influence.

At dawn Blauvelt Road was deserted. My brother and I walked down the street to Meisels's shul, weary after the Tisha B'Av service the previous night. We had lingered in synagogue until long past midnight, sitting cross-legged on the floor in our five-dollar Chinese slippers from Pathmark as the cantor wailed the Lamentations of Jeremiah. For four hours we contemplated the tragic event that defined Jewish history: the destruction of the First Temple, built by King Solomon. The Bais HaMikdash was a sanctuary for the *shechina*, "the mother of the soul," God's presence in the world. Miracles took place daily inside its walls, my brother explained. There was never a fly in the slaughterhouse; the smoke cloud from burning sacrificial offerings formed a straight pillar to the sky; and no matter how many Jews entered the Temple to pray, there was always room for more. But then the Jews turned to idol worship, sodomy, and murder. Man's evil inclination triumphed, and divine punishment ensued: the Babylonians under King Nebuchadnezzar razed the Temple to the ground and emptied the city of Jerusalem. "The Lord is in the right, for I have rebelled against his word," the cantor chanted. "But hear, all you peoples, and behold my suffering; my maidens and my young men have gone into captivity."

The First Temple's destruction was the first of a succession of tragedies that befell the Jews on Tisha B'Av. The Second Temple's toppling 650 years later, the massacre by the Romans of the Jews of the town of Betar, the expulsion of the Jews from Spain in 1492 also took place on that fateful summer day. The lesson was clear, my brother told me: "Obey the Torah or risk incurring the wrath of Hashem." Every generation that did not see the rebuilding of the Bais HaMikdash had failed in some way to live by God's law. "Israel," he said, quoting the Rambam, "will only be redeemed by tshuva." That was the primary lesson of Tisha B'Av.

"Only the tsaddikim really understand what we lost when the Temple was destroyed," he said. "They often cry when they think about it."

"Have you ever cried at Tisha B'Av?" I asked my brother.

"Never," he admitted. "We're too pampered in the exile. We have our houses, our air conditioners, our cars."

Rabbi Meisels's mikvah had turned chilly overnight. We took a quick dip together. Despite the countless holy baths I had taken with my brother over the past year, I still could not make the leap of imagination that equated this ritual with a purification of the soul. I saw only the dirty tiles, the rusting pipes, and the jugs of disinfectant; my brother could feel the pure waters of Eden washing over his nashama and coating it with a layer of protective ointment. Our baths in the mikvah were a continual reminder to me of the abyss of perception that would forever divide us.

Back home, he picked up his t'fillin bag and filled his leather briefcase with computer textbooks, a volume from the Gemorah, the Chumash, and his prayer book for the morning service. He stole a quick glance at his refrigerator door, where he had hung the latest homily from Avigdor Miller, a nonagenarian rabbi from Brooklyn who turned out a steady production of inspirational tapes and pamphlets. Along with his morning mikvah, my brother believed, the homily's prescriptions helped to protect his soul from the corrupting influences of Sodom. I scanned the instructions—Ten Steps to Greatness on a Small Scale. It was advised that each should be practiced daily.

1. Spend thirty seconds thinking about the afterlife.
2. Say at least once a day, "I love you, Hashem."
3. Every day, do one act of kindness that no one knows about.
4. Say something to encourage someone.
5. At one meal, say, or at least think, that you're eating with Hashem in mind only.
6. Be aware of the principle, "Man was created in the image of G-d."
7. Once a day, give a person a full smile.
8. Spend thirty seconds each morning thinking about the great gift of garments.
9. Spend one minute thinking over what happened yesterday.
10. Spend time thinking about Jerusalem during the days of the Holy Temple.

We rushed outside just as the seven o'clock bus pulled up to the corner of Blauvelt Road. The Monsey Trails bus company, owned by a Hasidic family in New Square, had recently settled the most bitter legal dispute in Monsey's history. It had been yet another clash between the religious and secular worlds. For nearly forty years the bus company had obliged men and women to sit on opposite sides of its buses. A curtain, or a *mechitzah*, was strung down the center to shield ultra-Orthodox men during prayers. But in December 1993 a non-Orthodox Jewish woman from Spring Valley named Sima Rabinovicz refused to change seats during the afternoon prayer on a commute from Manhattan. Rabinovicz—championed as "The Jewish Rosa Parks"— sued the bus company for sex discrimination. Eventually, the company agreed to remove the curtain from its buses and allow passengers to sit wherever they wanted. Extra minyan buses were laid on for male worshipers, including my brother, who did not feel comfortable being exposed to women during their prayers.

Rabinowicz's lawsuit was still a painful subject in the ultra-Orthodox community. To my brother, she was a troublemaker and an enemy of the "real" Jews. He would spit whenever he heard her name, an act meant to repel the "evil eye" that she had cast upon the ultra-Orthodox, bringing trouble into their house. She held a special place in his personal Hall of Shame—somewhere between Theodor Herzl, the founder of Zionism, and Hannah Fhima, the woman who had pressed charges of kidnapping against the Lev Tohor Rov. Rabinowicz, like the others, had shown contempt for the Torah, my brother said. "She'll be rotting for a long time in Gahennim."

But in my brother's world view, Gahennim, or purgatory, was hardly the worst punishment that a sinner could be sentenced to after death. The worst, reserved for only a few great criminals, was to be pursued for an eternity by the demonic incarnations of one's *aveirehs*, or sins. An endless circumnavigation of the world, with no possibility of a reprieve, was the fate of evildoers such as Adolf Hitler and Haman, who had tried to wipe out the Jews of Persia. My brother did not know what the world to come looked like. Unlike Christian conceptions of paradise, the Jewish idea of heaven is shrouded in mystery—but my brother believed he was bound for a magnificent place when his nashama left this earth.

The bus wound through Monsey and Spring Valley, the Hasidic driver calling men aboard with the chant of "Minyan, minyan." Passengers stood in the aisles, cloaking themselves in their tallises, tying on their t'fillin, and murmuring prayers. On the Palisades Parkway, a young Hasid with intense eyes behind clear spectacle frames rose in the rear and began to sing in a piercing baritone. All fifty passengers joined in, wailing and davening together as the bus rumbled through the banal sprawl of Paramus and the Meadowlands—past appliance warehouses, Chinese food pavilions, steak houses, Mexican cantinas.

But the prayer service had not reached its peak. As we entered the bus lane for the Lincoln Tunnel, two Hasidim unfastened the brass clasp of a plain wooden box in the rear. They slipped the Torah out of its blue velvet sleeve and held it up reverently for the other passengers to view. The Torah bearers began to sing from the Book of Deuteronomy, struggling to keep their balance as the bus rattled along the rutted highway. From other buses, secular commuters eyed the scene curiously. The Empire State Building, the World Trade Center loomed through the summer haze. The worshipers prayed on, oblivious.

From my seat against the window, I turned to observe my brother, who leaned over the Torah, chanting from the yellowing scrolls. He flashed me a knowing smile. He had initially recoiled from the idea of praying aboard a bus to New York, he had told me earlier—it seemed too jarring a collision of the sacred and the profane. But his first ride to computer class had changed all that. Now he saw the ritual as a blessed event: amid the humdrum reality of their workaday lives, he said, these Jews had managed to transform their rush-hour commute into a joyful journey into transcendence.

The service wound down as the bus plowed through the Lincoln Tunnel. The Hasidim rolled up the Torah, covered it in its sleeve, and laid it gently back in its box. And then, suddenly, we were in Midtown Manhattan. An army of commuters rushed along West Forty-first Street. We rolled past the Port Authority Bus Terminal, past three-card monte players, homeless men, young women wearing short skirts and tank tops. My brother turned his face away from the window. "I try not to look," he said. I disembarked at Forty-seventh Street, leaving my brother to continue his journey to Wall Street. Stepping onto Fifth Avenue, I removed my yarmulke as inconspicuously as possible and melted into the crowd.

SUKKOS WAS THE AUTUMN HARVEST FESTI-val, a time to rejoice in *shalom bayyes*—family harmony— and the bounty of God's many blessings. The holiday seemed to have special meaning this season. Nearly a year had passed since my first visit to Monsey, and my brother's life seemed to have progressed far from the nadir of the previous November. He was nearly halfway through his computer programming classes. Although his family had gone deeply into debt, a sense of order and stability seemed to have returned to the house on Blauvelt Road. There were no more visits to the Lev Tohor Rov—with whom my brother had celebrated a jailhouse Sukkos only two years earlier. He had even taken the time to drive the family to Arlington, Virginia, for a long weekend at my mother's apartment. The house had never looked better. New lighting lifted the perpetual gloom. Bright curtains, sewn by Ahuva during summer, adorned the windows. New beds and dressers gleamed in the children's bedrooms, and a fresh coat of pastel blue paint, with a stenciled pattern of birdcages, white picket fences and sunflowers cheered up the kitchen walls.

My brother was still as enamored of the Hasidic way of life as he had ever been, but he had given up trying to inflict it on the rest of his family. "Dovid is going to be Hasidic, and the two babies too," he had announced to me at one point that fall. "But the older three will be Litvishers. Ruchel will marry a nice yeshiva boy from Lakewood, New Jersey, and that's fine with me."

Sukkos comes at the end of the High Holy Days—a month-long period of spiritual elevation that begins with Rosh Hashanah, the Jewish new year. For me, it marked the ending of a cycle that had begun with my first visit to Monsey on a wintry November day the previous year. I had made eight trips to the village, experiencing life through the changing seasons, seen ultra-Orthodox life in the arctic winter in Canada and the dog days of the New York summer. My brother's own life seemed to have gone through as many permutations as the leaves that now covered Blauvelt Road. And my own impressions of him had evolved through shades of anger, frustration, empathy, and acceptance.

A light rain began to fall as I walked to my brother's house from the bus stop. Beneath the murky gray sky the village appeared, as always, peaceful. I found my brother and his family gathered inside a wood-paneled hut built onto the rear of his house. The sukkah commemorated the Jews' wanderings in the Sinai desert; the hut symbolized the clouds sent by God to protect them from the searing desert sun.

"Shalom aleichem, Yehoshua," he greeted me.

Rain trickled through the leaky roof made of woven bamboo sticks, puddling on the table and splattering on my brother's shiny new jacket. Biblical pictures tacked to the hut's walls had been covered with a protective layer of polyethylene. They had been painted by Ahuva many years ago: Joseph and the coat of many colors, David and the shield of Hashem, Aharon beneath the clouds of glory. The paintings bore the wear and tear of a dozen Sukkoses, and in their faded colors and water stains I saw the whole course of my brother's life in Monsey: the endless cycle of the holidays, the births of his children, the deepening fervor. I realized, suddenly, that my brother and his wife had now spent nearly half their lives in the hamlet.

The children gathered around me. Yosef Dov handed me an *esrog*, a bright yellow fruit, and a *lulav*, a date palm leaf tied together with myrtle and willow branches. Known in the Torah as the "four species," these Sukkos props are meant to symbolize the heart, spine, mouth, and eyes of man. Together we said a Sukkos prayer and waved the "four species" in four directions—up and down, from side to side—signifying the realm of God.

The next day—the last day of Sukkos—was the final opportunity of the year for Jews to repent and avoid possible eternal punishment. We would celebrate the holiday this year with Rabbi Meisels, whose own family had recently been dealt a serious setback. After just three months of marriage, eighteen-year-old Yosi had fled from his wife in Israel and come back to live with his parents in Monsey. Rabbi Meisels was distraught and embarrassed, Ahuva said. My brother was tight-lipped about the causes of the marriage's failure, attributing the breakup vaguely to the "different mentalities" of Israeli and American Hasidim—and to the infiltration of secular ideas into the once pure Jewish community.

Rabbi Meisels looked glum as he sat smoking a Marlboro in the sukkah attached to the porch of his old white house. Yosi sat beside him. The rabbi didn't mention his disappointment, and I did not think it tactful to bring it up. My brother and I were joined by a dozen Hasidic and Litvisher worshipers in the hut for almond cookies and cakes; then we all descended into the basement synagogue for the service. We formed a procession that circled around the Torah platform, waving our branches and fruits while chanting, "Hoshanah, Hoshanah." Save us, save us. After each revolution Rabbi Meisels stood before the Holy Ark of the Torah and blew sharp, bleating notes of a ram's horn. We beat our willow branches against the floor until all the leaves had fallen off, releasing the Almighty's essence from its symbolic containment in the branches, my brother later explained. Of all the many holidays I had celebrated at my brother's side, this one seemed the most esoteric. As I watched the men in black circling the synagogue, waving their palm stalks and fruits, and shouting, "Save me!" I felt as if I were witnessing some ancient pagan ritual.

During my year of visits to Monsey, friends had sometimes asked me if I found myself developing a new sense of spirituality. Not exactly, I would tell them. But there were moments, walking along Blauvelt Road from synagogue, when the fervor and certainty I had witnessed started to chip away at my skepticism. I could not help but feel awed by the survival of these ancient rituals in such elaborate exactitude. The very strength of this religious impulse seemed at times to suggest that some form of higher truth must exist. And the protective womb of the ultra-Orthodox environment made it somehow easier to believe in a benign deity.

Still, after the countless hours I had spent in shul, the mikvahs, the Sabbaths and Jewish holidays I had celebrated with my brother, I was no closer to believing in God. For my brother the Almighty seemed as tangible as the stones of the Wailing Wall of Jerusalem. Over the year he had become more and more hopeful that I would become reborn as a religious Jew. He gave me books—*The Ways of Tsaddikim, Response from the Holocaust, The Waters of Eden*, a pamphlet about the mikvah—and urged me to attend Sabbath services at an ultra-Orthodox synagogue in Los Angeles. He reminded me that Ohr Somayach had opened a West Coast branch. He even called early one morning to discuss some point about the Talmud and, midway through the conversation, reminded me to "wash *negel vasser*"—the ritual hand-washing ceremony, to remove the impurity from my soul that had crept in during sleep.

I wondered what would happen when my brother realized that I would never become a frum Jew. Would our relationship be able to sustain itself? Or would I be written off as a disappointment, a lost cause like my father, who had ignored "truth" for the false gods of science and the secular world?

I hoped that we would maintain some contact. I was sensing a growing connection to him. There were flashes of humor, vestiges of spontaneity and playfulness—especially around his children—that offered glimpses of the brother I had left behind in Jerusalem seventeen years earlier. But I knew that any reconciliation would have to be on his terms. My brother would never leave Monsey. Sometimes in shul I would spot an aging worshiper—rheumy-eyed and white-bearded—and see in him a vision of my brother forty years into the future. He would grow old here. His children—or most of them—would marry other members of the community, and in a few years he and Ahuva would become grandparents. I could easily see him now as a tsaddik, surrounded by grandchildren and great-grandchildren in the house on Blauvelt Road. He would be poor. And I supposed that he would be happy.

It was not my idea of happiness. I often felt that my brother was walking about in a state of permanent hypnosis. In exchange for the protective balm of absolute faith, it seemed to me, he had cut himself off from much of the richness and diversity of life. He talked incessantly about the joys of the ultra-Orthodox world—the yom tov, the Sabbath, the seder, the lulav and the esrog—but they sometimes seemed, from my secular vantage point, poor compensation for all that he had given up. He had woven himself into a coccoon, I thought. It was safe and warm, filled with its own satisfactions, the conviction that far greater joys lay in the world to come. What I had never realized before making my journeys to Monsey was that my brother was still on a journey of his own. His religious awakening was, I was sure, irrevocable. But it was a constantly evolving process, a reflection of his restless, searching personality.

Cold rain soaked my jacket and streamed down my face. It was the night after Sukkos, and my brother and I were walking to the village of New Square to celebrate Simchas Torah—the triumphant conclusion of a year's reading of the five books of Moses. My brother was feeling joyful. The High Holy Days were finally drawing to a close, and the last verses of the Torah would be read tonight. The following Sabbath the cycle would begin again. "Imagine you had a million dollars, spent it all, then discovered that you had another million dollars to spend," he said as a lone car splashed down Route 306. "God's gift of the Torah is infinite."

He seemed delighted that I had agreed to join him on this trek and would gain yet more exposure to upgegebenkeit, the pure love of God that defines the lives of the Hasidim. "Do you realize what a mitzvah this is, walking these six miles back and forth to New Square?" he asked me. We were walking because it was prohibited to drive on Simchas Torah. Fifty minutes later, we turned down Washington Street, the leafy main avenue of New Square, which was now a thriving community of five hundred pious families. Hasidim streamed from their apartment blocks and hustled along the rain-slick pavement toward the synagogue, where the charismatic Skvira rebbe would dance with the Torah until dawn. Their fedoras and streimels, I noticed, were covered with plastic garbage bags for protection against the rain. According to Jewish law, unfurling an umbrella is the equivalent of erecting a tent, my brother explained, and it is forbidden on Shabbos and Jewish holidays to build structures of any sort.

We passed Jackson Street, Jefferson Street, Lincoln Street, and Bush Street. In homage to his adopted country, New Square's first rebbe, Jacob Joseph Twersky, had named all the streets of his community after American presidents. My brother inhaled deeply as we approached the large white-brick shul.

"It smells like Israel," he said.

Tonight, for Simchas Torah, twelve-tiered wooden bleachers rose on all four sides of the hangar-like synagogue. The benches were mobbed with about three thousand Hasidic men and yeshiva boys. The women and girls were packed into a gallery high in the synagogue's rafters. It looked airless up there: they fanned themselves frantically with paper plates. There was a sense of giddy anticipation—like the mass delirium before a high school basketball championship game. The scene seemed to capture the strangeness, the intensity, and the euphoria of my brother's world more than any other event we had shared.

In the middle of the huge crowd of men I spotted a single black face framed by a streimel and peyyes. He was New Square's lone African American Hasid, my brother told me, who had been named Abraham following his conversion to Judaism in the mikvah. The nashama of Abraham, the first Jew, is thought to inhabit every convert, my brother said.

We forced ourselves into the third row of the already crowded bleachers. Little peyyes-wearing boys balanced themselves precariously on milk crates perched on the narrow wooden benches. Although gusts of cold air seeped in through high windows, the temperature in the packed hall quickly soared. The Hasidim kept streaming into the hall, sandwiching themselves into the crowd.

At midnight, the Skvira rebbe—stocky, vigorous-looking, with a full brown beard and black-framed spectacles—strode into the synagogue. He positioned himself in front of a high wooden table adorned with three blazing candles, and faced east toward the elaborately carved Holy Ark of the Torah. The rebbe was dressed entirely in black, with a pair of knee-high black rubber boots that seemed more suited to duck hunting than to dancing. In his right arm he lovingly cradled a miniature Torah, the size of a newborn infant, swaddled in a white satin sleeve. A stern-looking assistant chased back overeager yeshiva boys who leapt off the benches to touch him. Tentatively, the rebbe began to dance a little jig—a few tiptoes forward, a few steps back.

Sonorous chanting reverberated through the overheated shul. It seemed to energize the rebbe. He hopped and skipped more vigorously up and down the aisle, his left fist punching the air, as if reaching for the firmament; his right arm cradled the Torah. As his dancing grew more flamboyant, the chanting became more urgent and the crowds swayed from side to side in dizzying synchronicity. The rebbe's dance was unlike anything I had ever seen before. With limbs flailing in wild abandon, he seemed intoxicated. Yet each seemingly random movement, I sensed, formed part of an elaborately choreographed ritual of self-surrender. As I watched his face radiate with pure joy and yearning for closeness with God, I thought that I had finally begun to grasp what the Lev Tohor Rov had meant when he talked about upgegebenkeit—the total abandonment of the self to the divine. Across the tiers, the stomping of six thousand feet sent the brass chandeliers swaying dangerously above our heads. Soon the roof was shaking; the entire room was vibrating. The sound of religious ecstasy washed over me. It was impossible to resist.

Locking arms with my brother, I found myself chanting from the depths of my being, adding my voice to the all-enveloping incantation.

"Ay yay yay yay ay yay yay!" I sang. "Ay yay yay yay ay yay yay!"

Swept up in the hysteria, I was able to catch a glimpse of my brother's face. Tears were streaming down his cheeks. He was gazing at the rebbe as if he were staring into the face of heaven.

about the author

JOSHUA HAMMER, a longtime correspondent for *Newsweek*, has covered sub-Saharan Africa, South America, and the Balkans and is now the magazine's Berlin Bureau chief. He has also been a contributing writer for *Harper's*, *Outside*, and *The New Republic*. This is his first book.